TRYING

NEAIRA

TRYING NEAIRA

THE TRUE STORY OF A COURTESAN'S SCANDALOUS LIFE IN ANCIENT GREECE

DEBRA HAMEL

YALE UNIVERSITY PRESS
NEW HAVEN & LONDON

Designed by Mary Valencia.
Cartography by Bill Nelson.
Set in Meridien type by Achorn Graphic Services, Inc.
Printed in the United States of America by Integrated Book Technology

The Library of Congress has catalogued the hardcover edition as follows:

Hamel, Debra.
Trying Neaira : the true story of a courtesan's scandalous life in Ancient Greece/Debra Hamel.
p. cm.
Includes bibliographical references and index.
ISBN 978-0-300-10763-0(alk. paper)
1. Neaira—Trials, litigation, etc. 2. Trials (Prostitution)—Greece—Athens. 3. Prostitutes—Greece—History. 4. Apollodoros, b. ca. 394 B.C. Against Neaira. I. Title.

KL4115.6.N43 H36 2003
364.15'34'09385—dc21
2002029601

A catalogue record for this book is available from the British Library.

The paper in this book meets the guidelines for permanence and durability of the Committee on Production Guidelines for Book Longevity of the Council on Library Resources.

ISBN 0-300-10763-3 (pbk. : alk. paper)

10 9 8 7 6 5 4 3

For my fluffy-haired Rebecca

CONTENTS

CONTENTS

PREFACE

The prosecutor was in his early fifties, boorish and unattractive,
to judge by the description he had given of himself some ten
years before, and with a booming voice that carried well in the
court. It was early yet, an hour or two into a trial that would
last the rest of the day. The 501 jurors hearing the case were
not yet distracted by grumbling stomachs and the thought of
collecting their wages when the verdict was in. Apollodoros was
just getting started on his denunciation of the defendant, Neaira
(pronounced "neh-EYE-ruh"). "A bunch of them had sex with
her while she was drunk," he tells the jurors, describing the
aftermath of a dinner-party given some thirty years before.
"Even the slaves." And Apollodoros had the testimony of witnesses to substantiate the story. The lurid account of Neaira's
alleged youthful revelry was at best only tangentially related to
the prosecution's case. But in the Athenian lawcourts of the
fourth century B.C., relevance, and the truth itself, very often
took a back seat to a more urgent concern, rousing the jurors'
hostility, by any means possible, against one's opponent.

At the time of her trial Neaira was a foreigner resident in
Athens. "Foreigner" in this context means only that Neaira was
not an Athenian citizen. She had emigrated to Athens from
Megara, another one of the some 750 independent city-states

(or poleis, the plural of polis) into which Greece was divided at
the time. (The emergence of Greece as a united nation awaited
the Greek War of Independence in the early nineteenth century.) Neaira had grown up in another Greek polis, Corinth, in
the northeast of Greece's Peloponnese, but we cannot know
whether she was herself of Greek extraction: Corinth was a
flourishing center of commerce, and traders from throughout
the Mediterranean regularly passed through its ports. We know,
at least, that Neaira lived in Corinth from a very young age,
and possibly from birth. She would therefore have spoken Greek
fluently—but the Doric dialect of Greek that was prevalent in
the Peloponnese, not the Attic dialect of Athens. Neaira's speech
would have been perfectly understandable in her adoptive polis,
but unless she had managed in adulthood to change her pro-
nunciation, her accent would have distinguished her from na-
tive Athenians.

Neaira was born in the decade after Athens lost the Peloponnesian War to Sparta and the Peloponnesian League (404 B.C.).
(All the dates in the narrative are B.C. unless otherwise indicated.) By the time of the trial, sometime between 343 and 340,
she too was in her fifties. She had spent much of her life working
as a courtesan, her fate largely sealed when she was enslaved
as a child to a Corinthian brothel-keeper. But in many ways
Neaira had been successful. She had gained her freedom and
eventually settled into a thirty-year relationship with a certain
Stephanos, an Athenian citizen. The nature of that relationship
was the central question in her trial.

Apollodoros was attempting to show in his speech that
Neaira had broken the law by living with an Athenian citizen
as his wife (rather than, for example, as a mistress): at the time
of Neaira's trial, marriages between citizens and noncitizens in
Athens were illegal, though less formal relationships between
lovers were unproblematic. Conviction in the trial would result

in Neaira's enslavement—Athenian courts regularly imposed what most of us would consider impossibly harsh sentences—while Stephanos would be punished with a stiff fine, the equivalent of two or three years' worth of a skilled laborer's wages. Apollodoros was not particularly interested in destroying Neaira. Her enslavement, if he managed to persuade the jurors that punishment was called for, would merely be collateral damage in the feud he was pursuing with Stephanos: the two had faced one another in court before. Humiliating Neaira in public, dredging up—or inventing—sensational details about her past, was simply a means of retaliating against Neaira's lover.

We can be excused for taking pleasure, two and a half millennia after the fact, in Apollodoros' attack on Neaira. The speech he delivered in court has been preserved and is an important source of information about Athenian law and social history. It has something to tell us about a host of different subjects—prostitution, adultery, religious practices, slavery, enfranchisement procedures, private arbitration, homicide law, and so on. Not least, it has preserved for us most of what we know of Neaira's story, a rare view of a woman's life—admittedly an unusual life—in ancient Greece.

Apollodoros' speech is one of about a hundred Athenian lawcourt speeches that have survived completely or largely intact. Between roughly 420 and 320, speechwriters in Athens, probably several score of them, were regularly composing speeches for delivery by themselves or others either in court or before the Athenian assembly of citizens. (There was another recognized type of speech as well, however, the "epideictic," display oratory written for the amusement of an author's audience or for a public occasion such as the burial of Athenian soldiers.) Speeches written by or attributed to ten of Athens' speechwriters were collected in antiquity and preserved. The canonical authors, the so-called Ten Orators, are Aeschines, Andocides, Antiphon, Demosthenes, Dinarchus, Hyperides, Isaeus, Isocrates, Lycurgus, and Lysias. (We will be hearing more about the last of these men in Chapter 1.) A number of speeches attributed to the more distinguished orator Demosthenes are believed to have been written in fact by Apollodoros, Neaira's prosecutor, who is sometimes referred to as the eleventh Attic orator (by, for example, Lionel Pearson in the title to his 1966 article, "Apollodorus, the Eleventh Attic Orator"). In particular, the speech Apollodoros delivered at Neaira's trial was very probably composed by him as well. (There is general agreement that the following six speeches in the Demosthenic corpus were composed by Apollodoros: 46 *Against Stephanos II*, 49 *Against Timotheos*, 50 *Against Polykles*, 52 *Against Kallippos*, 53 *Against Nikostratos*, as well as 59 *Against Neaira*.)

Like any of the extant Athenian lawcourt speeches, Apollodoros' *Against Neaira* has to be used with care. Litigants in Athenian trials regularly distorted the information they presented to juries, misrepresenting the situations under discussion or indeed lying outright in order to achieve their purposes. A prosecutor might even misrepresent the law or laws at issue in a case in order to confuse jurors and exaggerate the defendant's culpability. This degree of prevarication may seem surprising: we in modern democracies are accustomed to a legal system in which trials are overseen by professional judges who instruct jurors in the correct understanding of the laws pertinent to a trial. But there were no professional jurists in Athens. What litigants could get away with in a courtroom was defined not by rulings from the bench but by the response of the jurors themselves, from supportive murmurs to heckling to questions shouted from the floor to the final verdict. We can assume that Apollodoros, like any Athenian orator, was less than truthful in his speech when he needed to be and when he thought he would not be found out.

This book tells the story of Neaira's life and of her family's experiences, culminating in Apollodoros' prosecution of her in the late 340s, with attention given also to the feud that occasioned the trial. Apollodoros' speech, inevitably hostile to Neaira, must be the principal source for her biography, though we will need very often to question and reject the information he provides. Where what he tells us is not inherently unlikely, however, or contradicted by other sources, and when lying about the issue under discussion would not have furthered the prosecution's case, we can feel reasonably confident about accepting Apollodoros' testimony. Fleshing out Neaira's story, too, will require frequent dips into other source material.

Any citations by section number alone in this book are to be understood as referring to Apollodoros' speech against Neaira (unless some other referent is obvious). All translations from the Greek are my own.

Konstantinos Kapparis (1999) and Christopher Carey (1992) both provide translations of the complete text of *Against Neaira* in their commentaries. A recent translation by Victor Bers of this and nine other speeches in the Demosthenic corpus can be found in the Oratory of Classical Greece series published by the University of Texas Press. Because *Against Neaira* was preserved in the Demosthenic corpus, texts and translations of it will almost invariably be found in compilations of his work (as speech 59) rather than under the name of Apollodoros. Readers may also be interested in Carey's *Trials from Classical Athens*, a selection of sixteen Athenian lawcourt speeches by various authors, with introductions and explanatory material.

Every classicist writing in a modern language about ancient Greece must decide what transliteration scheme to adopt— whether to write Peiraieus or Piraeus, for example, Eunikos or Eunicus. I follow the majority in opting for inconsistency. I use

Latinate spellings (c for k, -us for -os, etc.) for the more familiar terms and names while transliterating less well-known words directly from the Greek.

For the convenience of the reader, I summarize here the relationship among the ancient monetary units mentioned in the text:

6 obols	= 1 drachma
1 mina	= 100 drachmas
1 talent	= 6,000 drachmas

ACKNOWLEDGMENTS

I owe a great debt in writing this book to the recent commentaries on the speech by Konstantinos Kapparis and Christopher Carey. It may be assumed that every page of what follows has been informed by their studies, even where my debt to their work is not expressly acknowledged in the notes.

I am indebted as well to a number of friends, students, and colleagues who commented on the book or otherwise offered their help and advice. My thanks to Michael Behen, Carlotta Dus, Dina Guth, Gail Hoffmann, Wendy Karp, David Lupher, Kathleen McCarthy and her secretarial assistant Michael, Lisa McKenzie, David Seidemann, Laurie Shaner, Craig Williams, and the incomparably diligent David Whitehead. Victor Bers, who has midwifed my various projects for some ten years now, gave his unstinting help in this case also, for which I am, as usual, more than grateful. My thanks to Bill Nelson for his beautiful maps; to Glen Hartley, Lynn Chu, and Catharine Sprinkel for their work in getting the book to print; to Larisa Heimert, Keith Condon, Margaret Otzel, and Noreen O'Connor of Yale University Press for their editorial assistance; and to the publisher's anonymous readers for their thoughtful responses to the text.

Melissa Seidemann, finally, though she obdurately refused

to help with the text, was a sweet-faced, mostly uncomplaining companion during my last bout with the manuscript prior to publication. I am grateful to her and to her sister Rebecca, to whom this book is dedicated, for making everything else matter.

CHRONOLOGY

Most of these dates are uncertain. References to more detailed discussions concerning them will be found in the notes at appropriate points in the discussion.

YEARS	NEAIRA'S AGE	EVENT
404 B.C.		Athenians surrender to Sparta: end of Peloponnesian War
404–403		Reign of the Thirty Tyrants
403		Restoration of Athens' democracy
403		Lysias composes his *Against Eratosthenes* (speech 12)
400–395		Birth of Neaira
c. 394	1–6	Birth of Apollodoros
388–382	12–13	Neaira visits Athens with Lysias
c. 380	15–20	Birth of Theomnestos

YEARS	NEAIRA'S AGE	EVENT
378	17–22	Neaira visits Athens with Simos
376	19–24	Timanoridas and Eukrates purchase Neaira
374	21–26	Neaira purchases her freedom and moves to Athens with Phrynion
374		Pythian Games party at Chabrias' house
373–372	22–27	Neaira leaves Phrynion and goes to Megara
371	24–29	Battle of Leuctra
371		Neaira moves to Athens with Stephanos, possibly with one or more children
371–370	24–30	Phrynion attempts to hale Neaira into slavery; private arbitration
370–365	25–35	Philetairos' *Huntress* performed
370	25–30	Death of Pasion
369	26–31	Stephanos prosecutes Xenokleides for failure to serve

CHRONOLOGY

YEARS	NEAIRA'S AGE	EVENT
c. 369		Apollodoros delivers [Demosthenes] 52 *Against Kallippos* (Demosthenes' name is bracketed because his authorship of the speech is spurious)
368	27–32	Apollodoros serves as trierarch
c. 366	29–34	Apollodoros delivers [Demosthenes] 53 *Against Nikostratos*
365	30–35	Apollodoros serves as trierarch
362	33–38	Apollodoros serves as trierarch (again)
c. 362		Apollodoros delivers [Demosthenes] 49 *Against Timotheos*
c. 360	35–40	Apollodoros delivers [Demosthenes] 50 *Against Polykles*
c. 360		Death of Archippe
359	36–41	Philip II comes to power in Macedon
358–353	37–47	Phrastor marries Phano; he divorces her one year later, when she is pregnant with his son

YEARS	NEAIRA'S AGE	EVENT
357–352	38–48	Stephanos brings suit for maintenance against Phrastor; Phrastor initiates proceedings against Stephanos; they come to an out-of-court settlement
357–352		Shortly after divorce, Phrastor becomes ill; he recognizes Phano's son as legitimate and introduces the child to his phratry and *genos*
356	39–44	Apollodoros serves as trierarch
352	43-48	Apollodoros serves as *choregos*
355–350?	40–50	Epainetos found *in flagrante delicto* with Phano
355–350?		Theogenes serves as *archon basileus*; he marries Phano and divorces her soon after the celebration of the *Anthesteria*
c. 350	45–50	Demosthenes 36 *For Phormion* and 45 *Against Stephanos I* delivered; [Demosthenes] 46 *Against Stephanos II* delivered

YEARS	NEAIRA'S AGE	EVENT
348	47–52	Apollodoros proposes decree related to Theoric fund; Stephanos brings *graphe paranomon* less than a year later
348		Philip of Macedon captures and destroys Olynthus
346?	49–54	Stephanos prosecutes Apollodoros for murder
346		Stephanos serves as ambassador to Philip?
343–340	52–60	The trial of Neaira

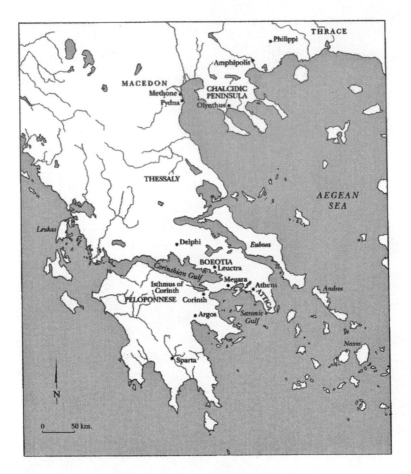

THRACE

Philippi

Amphipolis

MACEDON
Methone
Pydna
CHALCIDIC
PENINSULA
Olynthus

THESSALY

AEGEAN
SEA

Leukas

Delphi

Euboea

BOEOTIA
Leuctra

Corinthian Gulf

Isthmus of
Corinth
Megara
Athens

PELOPONNESE   Corinth
ATTICA

Argos
Saronic
Gulf

Andros

Naxos

Sparta

N

0   50 km.

GREECE IN THE CLASSICAL PERIOD

ATTICA

I

LIFE

AS

A

PROSTITUTE

I

NIKARETE'S

BROTHEL

Neaira grew up in a brothel in Corinth, a polis in Greece's Peloponnese famous enough for its prostitutes that the ancient Greeks made a verb out of it: *korinthiazein* meant "to fornicate." We cannot know what circumstances led to it—she may, for example, have been a foundling, left by her parents to be discovered and raised by others or to die of exposure—but Neaira was purchased when still a child by the brothel-keeper Nikarete, a former slave herself (and doubtless a former prostitute) who had somehow won her freedom. Nikarete reportedly had a knack for spotting potential in young girls. Apollodoros, in the speech he composed for the trial against Neaira some fifty years later, tells us that Nikarete "was clever at recognizing beauty in small children, and she knew how to raise them and train them skillfully" (§18).[1] Neaira was born, probably, in the early years of the fourth century, which suggests that she became a member of Nikarete's household in the 390s or early 380s. According to Apollodoros, she was prostituting herself already before she reached puberty (§22).[2]

Neaira was not the only girl in Nikarete's stable. Apollodoros names six others who were brought up and prostituted in the household, though they were not necessarily all contemporaries of Neaira: Anteia, Stratola, Aristokleia, Metaneira, Phila, and Isthmias (§19). Many if not all of these women were well known in their day. Several fourth-century plays were named after Anteia, for example, and the comic poet Philetairos mentions three of Nikarete's courtesans in his play *Huntress*, written probably in the early 360s. His remark is a joke about the advanced age at which some women prostituted themselves: "Didn't Laïs finally die fucking, and haven't Isthmias, Neaira, and Phila rotted away?" Philetairos presumably expected a large percentage of his audience to be familiar with the courtesans (*hetairai*) named, and the same may be said of Apollodoros.[3]

Nikarete, we are told, referred to Neaira and the other girls in her retinue as her daughters in order to maximize profits (§19): customers paid more for the privilege of sleeping with a free girl than with a slave. The charade was presumably one of many markers that distinguished Nikarete's prostitutes from the lower-class harlots of Corinth's sex industry: as we shall see, Nikarete offered her clients a quality product.

THE SEX-FOR-HIRE CONTINUUM

Prostitutes in ancient Greece—just as prostitutes in modern societies—came in a range of types, not neatly demarcated from one another, and prices. On the low end of the scale were the common whores or streetwalkers, the *pornai* (the word from which our "pornography" derives), who were very often slaves. (Pornai were also, therefore, usually not Greek: most slaves were imported into Greece from "barbarian" areas, that is, the non-Greek-speaking states that bordered the Greek world, from Thrace to the north, for example, or Caria in modern Turkey.) These pornai worked the red-light districts of Greece, dressed and made up provocatively so as to attract the attention of potential customers. Apart from having painted faces and suggestive clothing, some working girls, at least, wore shoes that advertised the business they were in: studs affixed to the soles of their sandals spelled out erotic messages—*akolouthei* or "follow me," for example—which were printed in the dust of Greece's unpaved streets as the women walked. A man who *did* follow might be led to some out-of-the-way place outdoors—an alleyway, for example, or some other semiprivate location—where for a small sum his hired girl would quickly take care of him.[4]

While some pornai "beat the earth" (*chamaitype,* or "earthbeater," was one name given to prostitutes) outside on the unforgiving ground, others worked out of brothels, likewise providing fee-for-service sex at low prices. In these establishments little or no attempt was made to maintain the pretense of respectability. The comic poet Xenarchos writes of brothels in which the prostitutes displayed themselves, "basking in the sun, breasts bared, naked and stationed side-by-side in a semicircle." Prostitutes were known also to try to lure customers by beckoning passersby from the windows and, perhaps, the roofs of their brothels—not the sort of thing respectable women would ever be caught doing. Note, for example, how unbecoming the orator Lycurgus thought the behavior of Athens' women was after the Athenians were defeated in 338 by Philip of Macedon: "When the defeat and the calamity that had occurred were announced to the people, and the polis was on tenterhooks over what had happened, and the people's hopes for salvation rested on those who were over fifty years old, it was possible to see free women at their doors, crouching down in terror and asking if their men were alive—some concerned about a husband, others about a father or brothers—appearing in a manner unworthy of themselves and of the city."[5]

Pornai charged their customers per sexual act. Prices varied depending on the prostitute and the services rendered. (The position assumed by the participants could also affect the price. The most desirable and most expensive of these was evidently the "racehorse," in which the woman sat astride the man.) (Figs. 1 and 2.) The cost seems to have ranged between one obol and a drachma or slightly more (there were six obols in a drachma), in other words, between about one-ninth and two-thirds of a

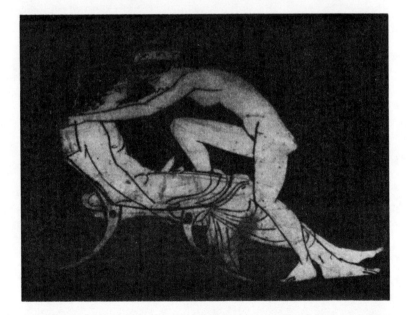

FIGURE 1. A woman climbs onto the lap of a willing male. The vase dates to the second half of the fifth century. Staatliche Museen zu Berlin—Preussischer Kulturbesitz, Antikensammlung/bpk; photo Jutta Tietz-Glagow.

FIGURE 2. An alternative position for the woman on top.
© Copyright The British Museum.

skilled worker's daily wage (assuming an average wage for skilled workers of one and a half drachmas).[6]

Also on the lower end of the scale were the *auletrides*—the term is conventionally (if incorrectly) translated as "flute-girls"—who entertained customers with music in addition to providing sexual release in return for payment: they played the *aulos,* a double-reed instrument which is thought to have sounded like an oboe (fig. 3). Auletrides regularly performed at symposia. These quintessentially Greek get-togethers were ritualized drinking parties at which males—no proper Greek woman could be present at such an event—entertained one an-

FIGURE 3. A flute-girl (second figure from right) pictured with other revelers, including hetairai. Martin von Wagner Museum, Universität Würzburg. Photo: K. Oehrlein.

other with conversation and song, and where they were themselves entertained by flute-girls and courtesans (fig. 4). Plato provides an account of one such party in his *Symposium*, but the festivities he describes are on the tame side: following the suggestion of one of the guests at the party, Plato's symposiasts send their flute-girl away and entertain themselves with conversation alone. The Athenian historian Xenophon provides an account of a less refined get-together at the house of a certain Kallias. The guests at Kallias' party, including the philosopher Socrates, are entertained by, among others, a flute-girl:

> When the tables were taken away and they had poured
> libations and sung a paean, a Syracusan fellow came in

for the entertainment. There was an accomplished flute-girl with him and an acrobatic dancing girl. And there was a very attractive young boy playing the lyre and dancing. . . . The flute-girl played for the guests, and the boy played the lyre, and both seemed to delight their audience particularly. And Socrates said, "By Zeus, Kallias, you have entertained us thoroughly. Not only did you give us a perfect dinner, but you're also providing us with the most pleasant sights and sounds."[7]

In Xenophon's account there is no hint of a potential for sexual intercourse with the performers, but the availability of auletrides for sex is made clear in Aristophanes' comic play *Wasps*. Toward the end of the play the character Philokleon brings a flute-girl away from a symposium with him with a view to getting her attention for himself. "Do you see," he asks her, "how cleverly I took you away when you were just about to suck off [*lesbi-*

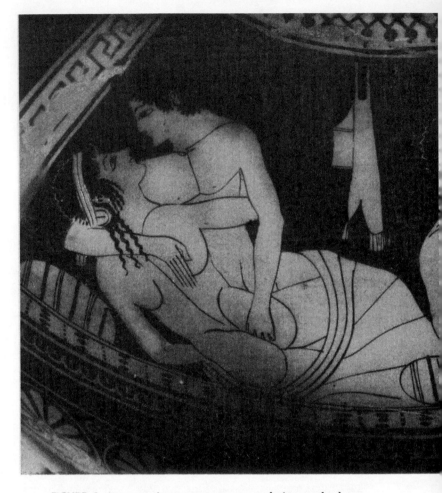

FIGURE 4. A symposium scene on a vase dating to the late sixth century. Musées royaux d'Art et d'Histoire—Brussels.

ein] the symposiasts?" According to Athenaeus in the *Dinner-sophists,* moreover, it was customary at symposia for flute-girls to be auctioned off late in the evening to the highest bidder.[8]

In fourth-century Athens, the maximum price that could be paid to flute-girls was established by law. Among the city's numerous officials were the ten *astynomoi,* whose duties included

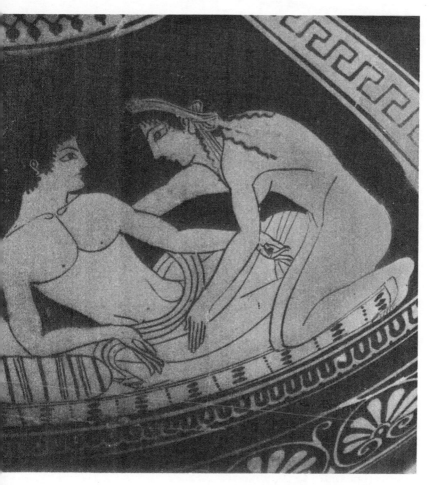

making sure that the flute-girls, the harp-girls, and the lyre-girls were not paid more than two drachmas for an evening's entertainment. "If a number of men are interested in hiring the same girl," the author of the *Constitution of Athens* tells us, "the astynomoi have the interested parties draw lots, and the officials hire her out to the winner." (The *Constitution of Athens* is a history and description of Athens' political system that was written in the late fourth century, probably by a student of Aristotle.)[9]

The need for such lotteries and for price-fixing suggests that there was severe competition in Athens for the services of flute-girls, or at least of *some* flute-girls. We may also imagine that the law was occasionally flouted. Indeed, in a speech delivered in the 320s the orator Hyperides mentions two men who were tried for having paid auletrides more than the price established by law. Presumably there were other scofflaws who were never found out: some flute-girls, at least, were probably able at times to bring home more than the top price allowed by law. It is also possible that sexual services were not included in the two drachmas that auletrides were paid for an evening's musical entertainment, or that sexual contact with the hired girls beyond some threshold required additional outlay.[10]

At the more expensive end of the sex-for-hire scale were women who were paid for a period of time—an evening or longer—rather than for a discrete sexual act. (Auletrides, admittedly, fell somewhere between these two categories.) These prostitutes were called hetairai, literally "female companions." They kept men company at symposia and other events, such as festivals, and entertained their clients with conversation as well as sex. Many hetairai were also musicians. They commanded much higher fees than the common pornai, with prices of ten drachmas and more per evening attested in our sources.[11]

In the case of the most elegant hetairai, the relation between services rendered and payment received was not made explicit: gifts were given to the women, favors were exchanged. The nature of the relationship between hetaira and customer was obscured, too, by the language used to describe it. In his *Memoirs of Socrates*, Xenophon tells of a meeting between Socrates and the courtesan Theodote. Asked by her guest to explain how she supported herself, Theodote only hinted at the nature of her business: "If someone has become my friend and wants to treat me well, he is my livelihood." Avoiding definition was a part of the courtesan's business. By not being obvious, by not, like pornai, blatantly offering themselves as commodities to be purchased, these high-class prostitutes maintained a fiction of respectability that increased the demand for their company. Significantly, the most successful hetairai differed from pornai also in that they were able to select the men on whom they would bestow their favors, and they had room to determine when and under what conditions a man's attention to them would be repaid.[12]

Neaira and her colleagues probably did not enjoy this level of freedom. As we will see later in this chapter, however, what we know of Neaira's life in Nikarete's brothel—the affairs she and her fellow prostitutes enjoyed with prominent men from throughout Greece—suggests that Nikarete's girls were among the more expensive and desirable of the city-state's prostitution circuit.

THE AVAILABILITY OF WOMEN FOR SEX

A man who was interested in engaging the services of a female prostitute in ancient Greece had a wide range of girls to choose from. (Male prostitutes were also readily available.) Prostitution itself, moreover, was perfectly legal. Indeed, prostitutes were taxed by the state in Athens, so little interest did the polis have in suppressing the industry. Buying sex from prostitutes, then, was sanctioned by law. It was also, on the whole, sanctioned by popular opinion. A man who visited prostitutes too frequently and squandered his inheritance on his pursuit of physical pleasures might be despised for his lack of self-control. But a Greek male need not have been ashamed of his judicious patronage of prostitutes. Where else, after all, was he to turn?[13]

Far more than in modern societies, where sexually liberated women regularly copulate with men to whom they are not married, prostitutes in ancient Greece provided a necessary service. Men who were in the mood to fornicate had a few options available to them. They could engage in homosexual sex with a male lover. They could seek gratification from one of the slaves of their household, male or female (an option which, however, may not always have been attractive, given that the slaves a man bedded would continue in his home indefinitely, rubbing elbows with his female relatives). Or they could buy sex from a male or female prostitute. Having sex with a respectable woman, for all but the most daring of Lotharios, was simply out of the question. Holding hands with a proper woman who was not a relative, for that matter, was hardly to be hoped for.[14]

The first problem the would-be lover of a respectable woman faced was an elementary one: how to get close enough to a potential paramour to make one's move. Free women who were not prostitutes were not easily approached on the street or in the marketplace. The women of ancient Greece were expected, ideally, to remain in their homes, spinning wool, overseeing the work of the household slaves, and in general attending to the many chores that needed doing in the home. (These generalizations do not apply, however, to Spartan women, whose society differed markedly from that of other Greek poleis, and who enjoyed far more freedoms than their counterparts elsewhere in Greece.) Even within the home, women were to have as little contact as possible with men who were not their relatives. If unrelated men were present in their house as dinner guests, for example, the women were expected to keep to the women's quarters of the house for the duration of the visit.[15]

The occasions when a man could get as much as a good look at an unrelated, respectable woman were few, but they did exist. Poorer women, for example, who had fewer slaves to run errands for them than the more well-to-do, presumably needed at times to see to tasks outside of the home. They may in fact have been compelled by their circumstances to work in public— selling ribbons in the Athenian marketplace, for example, as we know the mother of a certain Euxitheos was obliged to do in the mid-340s, a few years before Neaira's trial.[16] And even women who *were* successfully segregated from male society most of the time nevertheless had occasion to leave the confines of their homes once in a while. Greek women attended festivals. They grieved for their dead at funerals. And they sometimes visited with their neighbors. On such occasions they could be spied by strangers, and a man whose interest was sufficiently aroused by a glimpse of a woman in public could intrigue to see more of her, using, for example, a female slave—who would be free to walk the streets unaccompanied (unlike many respectable women, ironically enough)—as a go-between.[17]

But further complications awaited the man who had managed through intermediaries to arrange a rendezvous with a respectable woman: the logistics of the seduction itself. The comic poet Xenarchos, writing in his *Pentathlum* about the advantages of buying one's sex from a prostitute, notes that a customer in a brothel is never obliged "to set up a ladder and climb in secretly, or to get in through a smoke-hole under the roof, or to be carried in stealthily under a pile of husks"—the sort of tricks a man might use who was bent on satisfying his lust with another man's wife or daughter.[18]

Such escapades are the stuff of comedy, of course, and may seem improbable to the less adventurous of us. Surely the labor involved in spying out a respectable woman, arranging a rendezvous with her, and finally seducing her was not worth the payoff. Yet we know that assignations of this sort actually occurred. In one of the most interesting of the preserved speeches by the orator Lysias (*On the Murder of Eratosthenes*), we hear of a married woman who became involved in just such an affair. She was seen by a certain Eratosthenes, a man who allegedly made a habit of seducing respectable women, while she was at her mother-in-law's funeral. Eratosthenes subsequently paid court to her by using the woman's slave girl as an intermediary, and an affair ensued. As for comic aspects to their meetings, the couple allegedly entertained one another once on the first floor of her house while her husband was home, locked in an upstairs bedroom.[19]

The second problem facing would-be seducers of respectable women was that they could, when caught in the act (as Eratosthenes eventually was), be killed or otherwise punished by their lover's male guardian. We will discuss in Chapter 4 the sorts of punishments that an aggrieved head-of-household could inflict on a man he had caught in flagrante delicto with a woman in his charge. It will suffice for now to assure readers that the potential for punishment must have acted as an effective disincentive for all but the hardiest rakes. All things considered, it was far easier, and far less hazardous, for a man in need of sexual release to obey those suggestive, "follow me" footprints and slake his lust at the nearest brothel.

A CLIENT'S BIOGRAPHY

Among the men who regularly crossed the threshold of Nikarete's brothel was the very Lysias of whom we were just speaking, the speechwriter who composed *On the Murder of Eratosthenes*, which was delivered in court by the husband of Eratosthenes' lover after he was accused of Eratosthenes' murder (fig. 5). Lysias was a regular customer of Neaira's "sister" Metaneira. He played a small role in Neaira's drama, since he was the cause of what was presumably her first visit to Athens, which lay some fifty miles by land from Corinth.

Sometime probably in the mid-380s Lysias decided that he wanted to do something special for Metaneira. He had already spent a good deal of money on her, but he realized that whatever he spent was going directly to Nikarete, her owner. He decided he would bring Metaneira to Athens for the celebration of the Eleusinian Mysteries, a six-day festival sacred to the goddess

FIGURE 5. A bust of the orator Lysias—prolific speechwriter, victim of the Thirty Tyrants, and lover of Neaira's colleague Metaneira. Rome, Musei Capitolini (from a negative in the Archivo Fotografico dei Musei Capitolini).

Demeter, and he would pay for her initiation into the rites. The festival involved in particular a fourteen-mile procession from Athens to Eleusis, the town (deme) in Attica that gave its name to the celebration, and it culminated on the final day with an initiation ceremony. (We know next to nothing about this ceremony: initiates were required never to speak of its particulars, even to other initiates. This imposed silence explains why Demeter's festival was called the "Mysteries." The Greek verb *myein* from which the noun *mysterion* derived meant to shut one's mouth.)[20]

Lysias and Metaneira did not make the trip to Attica alone. Nikarete joined them, presumably wanting to keep a close eye on her investment, and Neaira came along as well. She was twelve or thirteen at the time and, we are told, already prostituting herself. Lysias put them up at the house of a bachelor friend of his, a sensible move given that Lysias was married and lived in the same house as his mother (§§22–23).[21]

It is worth discussing Lysias' life and career here in some detail. References to his work will crop up throughout our discussion of Neaira, and we can get an idea of the sort of client Nikarete's prostitutes attracted by looking at his example. Beyond that, Lysias lived through and played a role in some of the most dramatic moments in Athens' history. The story of his involvement in these events bears repeating.

Lysias lived in Athens as a metic, a free foreigner who could reside and work in the polis but who did not enjoy all the rights of citizenship. (Neaira would eventually have the same status in Athens.) His father Kephalos had moved to Athens from Syracuse (in Sicily) before Lysias' birth. The family was wealthy, making its money at least in part from a shield factory located in the Peiraieus, Athens' harbor area. They lived in the Peiraieus also, in a home Plato immortalized by using it as the dramatic setting for his *Republic*. In the introduction to that dialogue, the philosopher Socrates and a certain Glaukon (Plato's brother),

while visiting the Peiraieus, run into Lysias' older brother Polemarchos, who playfully badgers them into coming with him
to his father's house. Plato has Socrates describe the visit: "We
went to Polemarchos' house, and there we saw Lysias and Eu-
thydemos, his brothers. . . . Kephalos was inside too, Polemarchos' father. He seemed very old to me, because I hadn't seen
him in a long time. He was sitting on a chair with a cushion,
and he had a wreath around his head because he had been sacri-
ficing in the courtyard. We sat down next to him. Some cush-
ions were lying there in a circle. The moment he saw me Kephalos greeted me and said, 'Socrates, you don't come down to
the Peiraieus often and visit us. You ought to.' " It is a homely
scene, charming for its very ordinariness, and in marked contrast to what we know of the death, years later, of Lysias'
brother Polemarchos: he was executed at the hands of a short-
lived revolutionary government in Athens.[22]

After the Athenians surrendered to the Spartans in 404—
putting an end to nearly thirty years of fighting between these
major powers and their respective allies—the Spartans established in Athens a regime of thirty oligarchs, the Thirty, or, as
they were soon called, the Thirty Tyrants. During their brief rule
the Thirty were responsible for executing perhaps 1,500 of Athens' inhabitants. They did away with blackmailers (*sykophantai*)
and other scoundrels at first, then turned to more prominent
men, among them some of Athens' wealthier metics.[23]

We are fortunate in having a speech that Lysias composed,
probably in 403, for a trial against one of the Thirty. In it, Lysias
tells about the night he escaped death at the hands of the oligarchic government. He was entertaining guests, he tells us, when
some of the oligarchs came to his house. They drove off his
friends and handed Lysias himself over to Peison, one of the
Thirty. Lysias struck a bargain with Peison—his life in exchange
for a talent of silver, a small fortune that amounted to a decade's
worth of wages for a skilled worker in Athens. (A talent was

equal to 6,000 drachmas.) But Peison wound up stealing more than three times as much from Lysias' house, and though he assured Lysias that he would help him, he probably never intended to. As they were leaving the house, Lysias and Peison fell in with two others of the Thirty. These men took charge of Lysias, and Peison went off to see what he could find at Polemarchos' house.

Lysias was next brought to the home of Damnippos, an acquaintance of his. He was put under guard there with a number of others the Thirty had collected, but he managed to escape. When Damnippos went off to see if he could gain Lysias' freedom by bribing Theognis, the member of the Thirty who was guarding the house, Lysias ran out the back door. (A second exit was evidently an unusual feature in Athenian houses, which explains why the Thirty had not thought to guard Lysias' escape route.) Lysias writes:

> When Damnippos was talking to Theognis—I happened to be familiar with the house, you see, and I knew that it had a door in the back—I decided to try to save myself. I figured that if I got away I would be safe. If I was caught, and if Theognis had been persuaded by Damnippos to accept a bribe, I'd still be let go. And if Damnippos hadn't persuaded him, I'd be put to death just the same. With these thoughts in mind I fled. They had a guard posted at the door to the courtyard, in the front. I had to pass through three doors to get out the back way, and all of them happened to be open.
>
> I got out and went to the house of Archeneos, the ship owner. I sent him into the city to find out about my brother. He came back and said that Eratosthenes [one of the Thirty] had seized Polemarchos in the street and led him off to the prison. After I found this out I

sailed the next night to Megara. As for Polemarchos, the Thirty gave him their customary order, that he drink hemlock, without saying why he was to be executed— that's how far he was from getting a trial and being able to make a defense.[24]

In addition to losing his brother to the Thirty, Lysias also lost much of his property. He tells us that the oligarchs confiscated seven hundred shields from the brothers' factory in the Peiraieus, as well as the silver and gold, jewelry, furniture, and clothing that they took. One hundred twenty slaves, mainly factory workers, were seized by the state. And one of the Thirty, Melobios, had the audacity to rip a pair of gold earrings off of Polemarchos' wife when they raided his home.[25]

Fortunately, the Thirty did not hold power for long. They had installed themselves with the help of the Spartans in the late summer of 404. In the early summer of the next year they were defeated in battle by a band of democratic exiles under the Athenian statesman and general Thrasyboulos. Lysias, in exile himself at the time, helped the democrats by hiring several hundred mercenaries and providing the soldiers with perhaps two hundred shields. The Thirty were deposed soon after their defeat, and the oligarchic regime that was established in their place was itself soon out of power. In September 403 the various factions within Athens were reconciled and the democracy was restored.[26]

After the restoration, Lysias took up a career as a *logographos,* a writer who composed forensic speeches for clients who had to appear in court as litigants. He was a highly successful and respected writer, praised in antiquity as a master of style, and he was prolific: Lysias composed hundreds of speeches in the course of his career. Thirty-one of these have survived intact, along with numerous fragments from other speeches.[27]

FIGURE 6. The procession of citizens through Athens at the Panathenaia has been thought to be the subject of the Parthenon frieze. In this portion of the frieze, a bearded man receives Athena's folded robe from a child (or he may be giving it to the child). The goddess Athena is seated to the right. © Copyright The British Museum.

When Lysias brought Metaneira to Athens some fifteen years after the dramatic events described above, he was fifty years old or more. He had already lived through the "interesting times" the ancient Chinese are said to have cursed one another with. And he was regularly involved in Athenian lawsuits—for murder, for desertion, for impiety—in his capacity as speechwriter. The young prostitutes with whom he traveled in Athens and whose vacation he financed must have found him an intriguing travel companion.[28]

THE GREAT PANATHENAIA

Neaira visited Athens on another occasion as well, again under the observant eye of the brothel-keeper Nikarete. They traveled in midsummer, probably in 378, to attend the city's most important festival, the Great Panathenaia. This was the more elaborate version, celebrated every fourth year, of the Panathenaia, an annual festival in honor of the goddess Athena. People thronged to Athens from around Greece for the festivities—musical contests, chariot races, torch-races, a regatta in Athens' harbor, dancing by men in armor, sacrifices. Most famously, the Great Panathenaia featured a procession of citizens through Athens to the Acropolis, where the goddess Athena—or an image of her, at least—was presented with a new robe (fig. 6).[29]

Neaira and Nikarete were accompanied on their journey to Athens by Simos of Thessaly, presumably Neaira's lover. The evidence we have about the life of this Simos is fragmentary and difficult to interpret, but we do know that he was a member of the Aleuadai, the leading aristocratic family in the northern Greek state of Thessaly. He seems to have been a prominent citizen in Thessaly in the 350s, if not before, though it is impossible to know precisely what status he enjoyed at the time of his visit to Athens with Neaira.[30]

NIKARETE'S ESTABLISHMENT

The limited information we have about Simos' relationship with Neaira and Metaneira's affair with Lysias can yet tell us something about the sort of business Nikarete was running in Corinth. Her establishment, for one thing, attracted a Panhellenic clientele, not surprising, perhaps, given that Corinth lay at the western mouth of the Isthmus of Corinth (the narrow strip of land that separates central Greece from the Peloponnese) and that it controlled ports on both the Saronic and Corinthian Gulfs, on either side of the isthmus. Traffic by land between the Peloponnese and northern Greece necessarily passed through Corinthian territory, a boon for a business woman such as Nikarete, while sailors and merchants from around the eastern Mediterranean regularly passed through Corinth's several ports. Nor was Nikarete's clientele made up entirely, if at all, of working-class tourists and lustful sailors. Some of the men who patronized the brothel were prominent residents of their respective states. A client's relationship with one of Nikarete's prostitutes, moreover, was not necessarily confined to a single, fee-for-service transaction. It could become a more complicated affair, of long standing and perhaps infused with a degree of emotional attachment. Some interest beyond the purely sexual probably lay behind Lysias' desire to initiate Metaneira into the Mysteries. And Simos' relationship with Neaira, given his visit with her to the Panathenaia, is likely to have been similarly complicated.

Nikarete seems to have run an upscale establishment in the sex-for-hire continuum. Her women not only attracted prominent customers, but they held the interest of at least some intellectuals: Lysias evidently found Metaneira entertaining out-of-doors as well as in bed. Far from being paid per sex act, Nikarete's girls accompanied clients to festivals and dined with them at symposia: Apollodoros tells us that Neaira "drank and ate in the company of many men, as a hetaira would," when she visited Athens with Simos (§24).

Neaira became, we are told, something of a celebrity in Corinth (§26). When eventually she was sold—a subject about which more will be said in the next chapter—Nikarete received 3,000 drachmas for her, something like five or six years' worth of wages for a laborer. To put that in context, the orator Demosthenes tells us in a speech delivered in court in 364 that slaves working in his father's sword factory were worth between 300 and 600 drachmas apiece. Courtesans regularly cost more than other types of slaves, but even for a hetaira Neaira was on the expensive side.[31]

Neaira cannot be said to have been a hetaira of the highest class, however. She was, after all, a slave, working for a woman who presumably had the last word in how Neaira's relationships with clients would be conducted. "This Neaira," Apollodoros tells us, "was a slave of Nikarete's, and worked with her body, selling herself to anyone who wanted to get near her" (§20). She did not have the freedom of choice about her sexual affairs that the most celebrated hetairai enjoyed.

Neaira and her colleagues, according to Apollodoros, had undergone in their youth some kind of training at Nikarete's hands: "she knew how to raise them and train them skillfully," he says (§18). Fertile minds may leap to conclusions about their course of study, and Nikarete's prostitutes may indeed have required some instruction in technique to become adept at the trade: during the fourth century sex manuals proliferated, and a daunting range of sexual positions was evidently employed by professionals. Given the type of establishment they were being groomed to perform in, however, we may imagine that Nikarete's girls were educated primarily in conversational and other arts, talents with which hired women could charm men in social settings: customers of Nikarete's brothel were to be stimulated by deeds *and* words.[32]

DINING IN THE WOMEN'S QUARTERS

"Neaira," as we have already learned, "drank and ate in the company of many men, as a hetaira would," on the occasion of her second visit to Athens (§24). The remark would tell us a lot about the type of woman Neaira was even if Apollodoros did not explicitly label her actions as characteristic of a hetaira. The more obvious indication of her whorishness is the very fact that she dined with men. Respectable Greek women, as we have seen, had as little contact as possible with men outside of their families. "Married women do not go to dinner-parties with their husbands," the speaker of Isaeus' *On the Estate of Pyrrhus* tells us, "nor do they think it appropriate to dine with other men." Lysias provides an example of this kind of segregation in action in his speech *On the Murder of Eratosthenes*. Euphiletos, the cuckolded husband and defendant in the case, describes as follows the dinner he enjoyed with his friend Sostratos hours before he was himself to commit murder: "I ran into Sostratos after sunset when he was coming from the country. Since I knew that none of his friends would be home if he arrived at that time, I said he should have dinner with me. We went to my house and went upstairs [to the male quarters], and we had dinner." Euphiletos' wife was presumably in the house during Sostratos' visit (gussying herself up for the arrival of her lover, whom her husband would soon kill), but she kept to her own rooms: there was no question of her dining with her husband in the company of his male friend (fig. 7).[33]

FIGURE 7. A woman dining alone in the women's quarters. The pot
dates to the first half of the fifth century. © Copyright
The British Museum.

In another speech composed by Lysias, the defendant in a
trial for attempted murder complains about the behavior of his
accuser, a man by the name of Simon: "When he learned that
the boy [over whom they had quarreled] was with me, he came
to my house at night, drunk. He broke down the doors and went
into the women's quarters, where my sister and nieces were,
women who have lived so modestly that they are ashamed to
be seen even by male members of the family." The female relatives of the speaker, or so we are led to believe, were ideally

virtuous women: not content to feel shame before strangers, they were even squeamish about being seen by their relatives. In comparison with the behavior of these chaste exemplars of womanhood, Neaira's dinners with unrelated men, not to mention the brazen displays of bare-nippled pornai, would have been positively indecent—even had they not been a prelude to copulation.[34]

The second clue in Apollodoros' remark to Neaira's lack of respectability is the fact that he refers to her—and he does this throughout his speech—by name. Reputable women were very rarely mentioned by name in Athenian courtrooms. Instead, they were identified by their relationships to male relatives. We hear of "the daughter of Philonides," for example, or "Euktemon's wife, the daughter of Meixiades of Kephisia," or "the daughter of Polyaratos of Cholargos, sister of Menexenus, Bathyllos, and Periander." Speakers were more lax about their references to dead female relatives, but when a living woman is named in a court speech one of two things is virtually certain: either the woman was disreputable, or she was associated with the speaker's opponent in the case and he was referring to her disrespectfully because of that connection—perhaps with the idea of suggesting that there was indeed something less than proper about her.[35]

Neaira is named more than fifty times in Apollodoros' speech. She was a central figure in the case, of course, so avoiding her name would have required an acrobatic use of periphrasis. It *could* have been done, however, at least for the majority of the appearances of her name: in Demosthenes' speech *Against Onetor I*, Onetor's sister is referred to twenty-two times, not once by name. But doing his opponent the favor of not mentioning her by name was the last thing on Apollodoros' mind. What he most wanted, after all, was to impress upon the jurors trying the case the idea that Neaira was anything but a respectable Athenian wife.[36]

II

OWNERS

AND

OTHER

LOVERS

The life Neaira had known since early childhood in Nikarete's brothel could not last forever. As she grew older, Neaira's potential for future earnings decreased. Nikarete, naturally enough, would eventually want to rid herself of an asset that could only depreciate with time. In due course the opportunity to do so presented itself.

BUYING NEAIRA

Sometime after her visit to Athens with Simos, Neaira was purchased outright by two of her regular customers, Timanoridas of Corinth and Eukrates of Leukas (an island off the west coast of Greece) (§29). Apollodoros does not tell us in what year Neaira moved out of the brothel, but he does say that Nikarete sold each of the girls who worked for her "after she had profited from their youth" (§19). The "youth" to which Apollodoros is referring is probably the period during and immediately after puberty, "when the woman is, let us say, at the peak of her career," as one scholar puts it. We may guess, then, that Neaira was in her early twenties at the time she was sold, sometime in the mid 370s. Under different circumstances, had she been the free daughter of a typical Greek family, Neaira might have been married for several years by that time. As it was, instead of leaving her parents' household to join that of a husband, she left behind Nikarete's brothel and became the sex slave of two former clients.[1]

We have seen already that Neaira commanded a high price. Timanoridas and Eukrates pooled their resources in order to afford the 3,000 drachmas Nikarete was asking. Despite the enormous expense, purchasing Neaira was for them a cost-cutting measure. We are told that they had been required to pay "all the daily expenses of [Nikarete's] household" during the time they were buying Neaira's company (§29). Now they could use Neaira whenever they wanted, and they could expect to get back some of their investment when eventually they sold her off.

The relationship between the two owners of Neaira may seem curious to us, but it was not unique. In Lysias' speech *On a Premeditated Wounding*, written for delivery by a man charged with that offense, we hear of just such an arrangement: "The woman is joint property, both of us equally having paid money," the defendant tells us. He is talking about an arrangement he had made with the man now prosecuting him. "I paid the same amount of money for her." In the case of Lysias' client, shared ownership of a slave girl became problematic. "Sometimes she says she thinks more of me," he tells the jury, "and sometimes she says him, because she wants to be loved by both of us." Hostility over the girl culminated in violence, merely a black eye, according to the defendant, but attempted murder as far as the prosecutor was concerned.[2]

The outcome of the arrangement these litigants had made in happier days is perhaps not surprising. On the face of it, joint ownership of a single prostitute would appear to be fraught with the potential for jealous rages. In a society in which free, unmarried women were off-limits as sexual objects, it was not unusual for men to become infatuated with the women who *were* available to them. Resultant jealousies were natural enough, particularly as the love objects in question were prostitutes whose favors were theoretically available to anyone (fig. 8). At the least, one would expect petty complaints to arise, as might happen over the use of a jointly owned car or summer home. But Timanoridas and Eukrates appear to have made a success of it. We are not told of any problems developing because of their relationship, and the termination of their arrangement was evidently amicable and agreeable to all parties, including Neaira herself.

LIQUIDATING NEAIRA

After Timanoridas and Eukrates had enjoyed Neaira's full attention for some time, perhaps a year or more, one or both of them were ready to get married—not to Neaira, of course (§30). The partners decided to dissolve their arrangement at this point, whether out of some sensitivity on behalf of the wife or wives who were coming into the picture, or because of simple financial considerations: it was expensive to keep a courtesan, and money was tied up in her that could be liquidated and used for other more pressing purposes. They offered Neaira a deal. She could purchase her freedom from them for 2,000 drachmas, 1,000 less

FIGURE 8. The boy in the background has probably been beaten. The scene may depict a fight over the prostitute who is kissing the reclining man's hand. Martin von Wagner Museum, Universität Würzburg. Photo: K. Oehrlein.

than they had paid for her, on the condition that she leave Corinth. They told her, according to Apollodoros, "that they did not want to see her—she who had been their hetaira—working in Corinth or being under the thumb of a brothel-keeper" (§30).[3]

Apollodoros suggests that Neaira's owners were offering her a generous deal and that they were motivated in doing so by their regard for her. Brothels were notoriously unpleasant places for the girls employed in them, and brothel-keepers were notoriously unpleasant characters. Nikarete herself, Neaira's first owner, may have been a grasping mistress, but her upscale prostitutes were at least working out of a higher-class establishment than the brothels in which common pornai did business. Timanoridas and Eukrates, we are told, wanted to save Neaira from ending up in either kind of place.[4]

Neaira's owners may indeed have made their offer out of compassion for her, but there is another way to read the evidence. We cannot be certain that the deal they offered—her freedom for 1,000 drachmas less than they had paid—was indeed generous. Certainly, Apollodoros portrays it as magnanimous: "They told her . . . they would be happy to take less money from her than they had paid, and to see her getting some benefit. They said they would take 1,000 drachmas off the price of her freedom, 500 from each of them" (§30). But what Apollodoros has to tell us about the rationale behind their proposal— that they wanted to see her "getting some benefit"—is close to useless: he is openly hostile to Neaira, speaking about events that occurred in another polis some thirty years earlier; his phraseology suggests that he has knowledge of a conversation to which he was not privy, and that he is familiar with the motivations of men he is unlikely ever to have met. We should disregard his portrayal of the partners' offer as a generous one. For the same reason, whether Timanoridas and Eukrates were in fact very concerned with keeping Neaira out of a brothel must remain an open question.

The assumption that Neaira's owners were offering her a generous deal presupposes that they could have sold her to another party for more than 2,000 drachmas. But could Neaira indeed have fetched a higher price on the open market? She was in her twenties by this time, past her prime. Nikarete had sold her off not only because Timanoridas and Eukrates were interested in buying her, but because Neaira was no longer young. Chances are, Nikarete's competitors in the upscale sex-for-hire business were likewise only interested in maintaining younger prostitutes. The brothel-keepers who ran low-end houses, on the other hand, would doubtless have been interested in purchasing Neaira, but perhaps not for as much as 2,000 drachmas. Common pornai, as we saw in Chapter 1, were paid between one obol and one drachma per sex act. Even if Neaira were consistently paid the higher price for her services, she would not start turning a profit for her owner until she had produced 2,000 male orgasms—more if we take into account the percentage of the proceeds that went toward Neaira's upkeep. Brothel-keepers, too, were known for their avarice. We may imagine that they were hard bargainers, the used-car salesmen of antiquity. Could Timanoridas and Eukrates have expected to get the better end of a deal if they tried to hawk Neaira to one of these operators?[5]

What our partners really needed in order to fully recover their investment were buyers like themselves, not professional pimps but men who were so besotted with Neaira that they would pay top dollar for her. But finding precisely the right customer or customers could take time—more, perhaps, than Timanoridas and Eukrates could afford to spend on the project. All things considered, it was easier for them to do business directly with Neaira. They were certain of getting their price, and they were spared the trouble of haggling with hard-nosed pimps in Corinth's seedier districts.

Timanoridas and Eukrates, then, may not have been doing

OWNERS AND OTHER LOVERS

themselves any disservice by offering to sell Neaira her freedom for 2,000 drachmas. The deal they proposed was probably fair enough, however, beneficial for Neaira as well as themselves, at least as far as the price was concerned: we have yet to consider the implications of the strings they attached to Neaira's freedom.

Apollodoros tells us, as we have seen, that Neaira's owners did not want to see her working in Corinth when she was free (§30). They sold her her freedom, he says elsewhere, "on the condition that" she not work in their polis (§32). This proviso seems to have been a legal condition of her manumission rather than just an informal understanding arrived at by Neaira and her owners. Certainly Neaira acted as though the proviso had some legal bite to it. Apollodoros tells the jurors about a difficult two years Neaira spent in Megara, a polis on the Isthmus of Corinth, not long after she was freed. By way of explaining her continuing in a place where she could barely support herself, he says that "it was not possible for her to go back to Corinth, because she had got away from Eukrates and Timanoridas on the condition that she not work there" (§36). The implication is that Neaira would have gone to Corinth if not for the proviso. Apollodoros, of course, cannot be trusted to have accurate knowledge of the reasoning behind Neaira's choice of locales. But there is no obvious reason why he should lie when reporting the simple facts of her various moves from polis to polis: Neaira evidently never returned to Corinth, a large city in which she could expect to find work, which suggests that she took the stipulation on her freedom seriously. Her careful adherence to the clause in turn suggests that failure to comply with it would have been in some way punishable.[6]

We should not be surprised that Neaira's freedom had strings attached. Conditional manumissions were common enough in the period. But the proviso Timanoridas and Eukrates settled on was an unusual one. Most frequently, slaves were required as a condition of their release to stay on with their former owners for a specified period of time. Far from demanding more of Neaira's company, however, her owners never wanted to see her again. What is surprising, then, about Neaira's manumission is that Timanoridas and Eukrates were so very serious about keeping her out of their polis.[7]

It is not clear why they wanted Neaira to leave town. One scholar writes that she would have been "a perpetual reminder of their wilder days" had she remained. Perhaps so, but why should that have mattered? Were they purging the city of evidence of their sexual past, hoping to allay the jealousy of a future spouse or spouses? More likely, were they discarding Neaira because the male relatives of their future brides objected for some reason to her continued presence?[8]

The fourth-century comic poet Epikrates suggests another possible explanation for the proviso. Epikrates wrote a play called *Anti-Laïs* in which he describes the graceless old age of the notorious hetaira Laïs. He compares her to eagles that have grown old. After a youth spent devouring prey with the best of predators, these old birds are reduced to petty theft: "They sit on the temples of the gods, terribly hungry," waiting for a chance to steal scraps of food left behind on the altars. The aged Laïs is likewise brought low: "When she too was a young chick, she was made wild by the riches, and you could have seen Pharnabazos [we might say, with the same effect, the queen of England] sooner than her. But since she has run her course and her body is sagging, it is easier to see her than to spit. She flies off to every engagement, and she takes a half drachma in payment. She will give herself to old and young alike. Laïs has become so tame, my dear fellow, that she takes money right out of your hand." We need not imagine that Epikrates' depiction of Laïs is accurate. He was, after all, writing a comedy. But it is reasonable to suppose that he is describing a realistic type of woman: a formerly elegant prostitute who, as she ages, becomes less attractive, less expensive, and less particular. Perhaps Timanoridas and Eukrates, in disposing of Neaira so thoroughly, were taking precautions against the day when Neaira's attractions would no longer suffice to support her: they were unwilling to have underfoot a woman to whom, because of their former relationship, they might feel some obligation.[9]

PASSING THE PLATE

Neaira, of course, did not have 2,000 drachmas or anything like it. But she did have friends, or "friends," we might say, former clients on whom she could call for help. Apollodoros says that she "summoned them to Corinth" (§30), as if they might all have descended on the polis with money in hand (a muster of former suitors convened for the redemption of yet another promiscuous woman). On the face of it this is unlikely. Probably she wrote to a number of potential benefactors asking for money and "summoned" to Corinth the one from whom she could expect the most help. We see, at any rate, two observations we have made about the character of Nikarete's brothel here illustrated. Prior to her period of exclusive intercourse with Timanoridas and Eukrates, Neaira had catered to a Panhellenic clientele, not merely to residents of Corinth, and her relationships with men were, often if not exclusively, long-standing affairs rather than anonymous sexual performances. Otherwise Neaira would not have been able to contact her former customers, and they would surely not have been willing to help her financially.[10]

But Neaira's clients came through for her. A number of them sent her money—there does not seem to have been any expectation that she would pay them back—and one of them, a certain Phrynion, answered her summons and arrived in Corinth, laden with drachmas and eager to help a courtesan in distress. Neaira handed over to Phrynion the money she had collected from her other clients and as much as she had herself.

He, acting as her representative, gave it in turn to Timanoridas and Eukrates in the presence of one or two witnesses, adding the balance of what was needed himself §§31–32). Probably Phrynion paid the lion's share of the 2,000 drachmas. Certainly he acted afterward as if Neaira owed him something.[11]

PHRYNION'S ATHENS

When Apollodoros first mentions Phrynion in his speech, he says that Neaira's savior was "a man who was living his life extravagantly and expensively, as the older ones among you jurors remember" (§30). There are surely some racy stories hiding behind these words, but unfortunately they are lost to us. We know nothing about Phrynion's exploits before he fetched Neaira from Corinth. Still, Apollodoros' characterization is credible: what we are told of Phrynion's subsequent behavior and of Neaira's response to it suggests that he was indeed a man of immoderate temperament and appetites.

Phrynion was an Athenian citizen who came from, or whose family had originally come from, the village of Paiania in Attica, which lay about seven miles east of the city of Athens. Attica, the region which constituted the polis of Athens and in which Athens itself was the principal urban center, was divided into 139 such geographical units, or demes, of varying size. (Attica in the classical period covered an area of about 965 square miles, smaller than the state of Rhode Island.) Attica's demes were the building blocks of the Athenian political system, and every Athenian citizen belonged to one. An Athenian was fully identified by his name followed by the name of his father and that of his deme. The wealthy and licentious rescuer of courtesans who returned to Athens in 374 or thereabouts with Neaira on his arm was, properly introduced, Phrynion, son of Demon, of the deme Paiania (*Phrynion Demonos Paianieus*).[12]

Apollodoros gives us a taste of the life Phrynion and Neaira

briefly shared: "When he brought her back to Athens his behavior
toward her was outrageous and unrestrained. He went with her
everywhere to dinner parties, wherever he drank, and he always
went carousing with her. He had sex with her in public whenever
he wanted, everywhere, showing off the license he took with her
to anyone watching" (§33). Neaira, of course, was accustomed
to selling her body, and she had not been free while a slave to
select as lovers only those men who appealed to her. Her line of
work, in other words, had implied a measure of humiliation. We
need not suppose, however, that she was for that reason in the
habit of submitting to men in public: the Greeks seem to have
considered it shameful to be seen while having sex. Phrynion
may indeed have crossed a line when he had sex with Neaira in
front of an audience, making a show of her subjection to him.[13]

Apollodoros provides detailed information about one particular party that Neaira and Phrynion attended (fig. 9). It was
given in the late summer of 374 by Chabrias of the deme Aixone. Chabrias was celebrating his victory in the Pythian Games,
one of Greece's Panhellenic athletic competitions, of which the
most important was the Olympics. (The Pythian Games were
held every four years in Delphi in central Greece, the site of the
famous oracle to the god Apollo.) "Phrynion went with Neaira
to parties at many houses, including that of Chabrias of the
deme Aixone when he won with the four-horse chariot at the
Pythian Games in the archonship of Sokratides [i.e., mid-374 to
mid-373]. Chabrias had purchased the chariot from the sons of
Mitys the Argive. When he returned from Delphi he gave a victory feast at Kolias [just southwest of Athens, a promontory on
the Bay of Phaleron]. There, many of the guests—and even the
slaves who had served Chabrias' feast—had sex with Neaira
while she was drunk and Phrynion was sleeping" (§33).

The Chabrias who threw the party at which Neaira was allegedly so roundly used was a leading figure in Athens. During
his lifetime he served at least twelve times as a general, one of

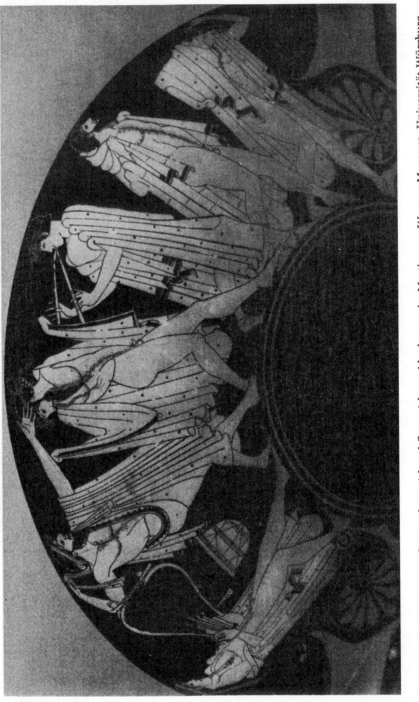

FIGURE 9. Partygoers reveling. A lyre-girl and flute-girl provide the music. Martin von Wagner Museum, Universität Würzburg. Photo: K. Oehrlein.

ten members of Athens' annually elected board of generals. (The generalship was the most important office in the polis.) By the time of his victory at Delphi in 374, Chabrias had been elected to the generalship at least five times. While in office in 376, in particular, he won an important victory over the Spartans at Naxos, one of the Aegean islands. Because of his victory the Athenians put up a statue of Chabrias in the agora and granted him *ateleia,* exemption from a sort of taxation that fell on Athens' more wealthy citizens. Once again, and despite those slaves at the party, Neaira was hobnobbing with the rich and famous.[14]

During Neaira's trial, Apollodoros introduced to the court witnesses to the debauchery that had allegedly occurred at Chabrias' house some thirty years before. (At the time of Neaira's trial, witnesses called by the litigants were present in the court, but they did not give evidence orally, as they had previously. Instead, a statement that was prepared ahead of time was read out by a clerk, and the witness confirmed the deposition's accuracy.) Apollodoros may, of course, be lying about the incident, and he may have suborned witnesses to back up his story. We cannot know for certain whether Neaira in fact consented while drunk to the advances of mere slaves. But whether the details Apollodoros provides are true or not, I think we get from his account a good enough sense of the sort of life Neaira was living in Athens. We can believe that she was ill-treated by Phrynion, because it was, if anything, counterproductive for the prosecution to portray her as Phrynion's victim. Apollodoros is most unlikely to have fabricated details that rendered her a sympathetic figure. As her subsequent actions indicate, moreover, Neaira was not pleased with the lifestyle Phrynion offered her.[15]

THE MEGARIAN YEARS

A year or a little longer after the victory party at Chabrias' house, between the summer of 373 and the summer of 372,

Neaira packed her bags and left Phrynion for the polis of Megara, roughly midway between Athens and Corinth. Unfortunately for Phrynion, some of the things Neaira filled her bags with were his. Apollodoros describes the move: "Since she was wantonly mistreated by Phrynion and not shown affection as she had expected to be, and since he did not do for her the things she wanted, she packed up some of his belongings from the house and all the clothing and jewelry she had got from him, and taking [her slaves] Thratta and Kokkaline with her, she ran off to Megara" (§35).

Under other circumstances, Neaira might have found Megara a pleasant haven. The polis was a center for prostitution which, like Corinth, attracted its share of traveling dignitaries. But in 372 there was a war on. Athens and her allies in the Second Athenian League had been fighting with Sparta since 378, trying to prevent the Spartans from suppressing the autonomy of the allied states. (In 378, some four years before Neaira attended his party, Chabrias had commanded troops in Boeotia, the region bordering Attica to the northwest.) Megara was right in the thick of things, perched on the land route between Boeotia and Sparta, the dominant polis of the Peloponnese. As Apollodoros explains in his speech, the war, not surprisingly, had a depressing effect on Megara's prostitution industry: "Neaira stayed in Megara for two years, during the archonships of Asteios [mid-373 to mid-372] and Alkisthenes [mid-372 to mid-371], but prostitution did not bring in enough money for her to support her household. She was extravagant, and the Megarians were mean and stingy. There also were not very many foreigners there because of the war and because the Megarians were supporting the Spartans while you [Athenians] were in control of the sea" (§36).[16]

The Boeotian War, as these hostilities are called, culminated in the summer of 371 with the battle at Leuctra, in Boeotia. There the Boeotian infantry, deployed in an unprecedented battle formation and using revolutionary tactics, wedged its left wing into the enemy's right and decimated the ranks of the elite Spartan troops posted there. When the battle was done, a quarter or more of Sparta's fully enfranchised men lay dead. Sparta's power was shattered as a result, and the way was paved for later Boeotian forays into the Peloponnese itself.[17]

The Battle of Leuctra significantly altered the balance of power in the Greek world. On a smaller scale, with Sparta's defeat and the cessation of hostilities in Greece there came also a significant change in Neaira's circumstances.

II

STEPHANOS
AND
THE
CHILDREN

III

SONS

AND

CITIZENSHIP

IN

ANCIENT

ATHENS

After the Battle of Leuctra, Neaira met another Athenian, Stephanos, son of Antidorides, of the deme Eroiadai. He came to Megara and stayed at Neaira's house, evidently for an extended period, and spent part of his time having sex with his hostess and part listening to the story of her life: "She told him about everything that had happened and about Phrynion's outrageous behavior toward her," Apollodoros tells us. Neaira took advantage of the opportunity Stephanos presented. She wanted to live in Athens, we are told, but because of Phrynion, still seething over her disappearance two years before with his belongings, she could not take up residence there on her own: "She was afraid of Phrynion because she had wronged him and he was furious with her, and she knew he had a violent and reckless disposition." But Stephanos could offer her some protection. By the time he was ready to leave Megara, Neaira had sold him on the idea of taking her with him to Athens (§37).[1]

SPONTANEOUS GENERATION

At this point in his narrative Apollodoros springs a surprise on us: when Neaira left Megara with Stephanos, he says, she had three children in tow, two sons, Proxenos and Ariston, and a daughter (§38). The daughter's given name was Strybele, but when she was older she came to be called Phano, and that is how Apollodoros regularly refers to her in his speech. According to Apollodoros, Phano came to rival Neaira in the salaciousness of her activities. We will have cause to discuss her conduct in much more detail in subsequent chapters. For the present we need only marvel at the children's sudden appearance in the story and consider whether Apollodoros is telling us the truth about them.[2]

If Neaira *did* have three children when she moved back to Athens after the Battle of Leuctra, where had they come from? It is unlikely that she was either (conscious of being) pregnant or already a mother when she was sold by Nikarete to Timanoridas and Eukrates in 376 or so. Pregnancy was surely an undesirable state for any of the girls who sold their bodies in the streets and brothels of ancient Greece. Apart from any consideration of the formidable risks that were associated with childbirth in the premodern era, a working girl's income depended on the maintenance of her appearance. Becoming pregnant would have been problematic in particular for Nikarete's girls, who were selling not only their bodies but also the illusion of respectability: Neaira could scarcely have played the virginal coquette with a swelling belly. Various oral contraceptives and early-stage abortifacients were in use during the period, and they seem to have been effective to some degree. Prostitutes, of all people, were surely in the know when it came to using them to prevent or terminate unwanted pregnancies. We can be confident that Nikarete did whatever was necessary to safeguard her business: the high-class courtesans of her brothel were not allowed to jeopardize their salability—or rentability—by becoming or remaining pregnant.[3]

Neaira, of course, may have been in the very early stages of pregnancy when she moved out of Nikarete's brothel, and if not, any one of a number of men could have impregnated her thereafter—Timanoridas, Eukrates, Phrynion, or any of the partygoers Neaira allegedly entertained at Chabrias' victory celebration. It was certainly physically possible for Neaira to have borne three babies between 376 and 371, when she moved to Athens with Stephanos. But Apollodoros can offer us very little evidence that the boys, at least, were Neaira's. As we will see, moreover, the prosecution had every reason to lie about the parentage of these children.

RAISING CITIZENS

Apollodoros is prosecuting Neaira because, he alleges, she, an alien, had broken the law by living with an Athenian citizen as his wife. In support of this contention Apollodoros attempts to prove two things to the jury: first, that Neaira was indeed an alien, and second, that Stephanos had been living in a marriage relationship with her. Apollodoros' account of Neaira's early life in Nikarete's brothel is part of his proof of the first contention. As proof of his second claim Apollodoros offers evidence that Stephanos acted toward Proxenos, Ariston, and Phano as if they were Athenian citizens. How Stephanos' treatment of the children could reflect the nature of his relationship with Neaira will be considered in a moment.

Apollodoros does in fact succeed in showing that Stephanos has treated the children as citizens. In the case of the male children, this means two things: first, that Stephanos presented the boys, probably at the age of three or four, to his phratry, one of the hundred or more kinship groups to which most Athenian male citizens belonged; and second, that Stephanos had their names inscribed on his deme's population register when they came of age at eighteen. As for Phano, Stephanos treated her like a citizen when he twice married her off to citizen males.[4]

Enrollment in the phratries and demes was the prerogative of citizens only. Thus Stephanos could not legitimately have introduced the boys to these associations if Neaira were their mother. Nor could he have legally given Neaira's daughter in marriage to an Athenian citizen. Since the mid-fifth century, Athenian citizenship (except in rare cases when noncitizens were enfranchised by special vote of the assembly) had been restricted to children whose parents were both Athenian citizens. Any child of Neaira's, therefore, even if Stephanos were the father, would necessarily not have been a citizen.[5]

Stephanos, then, raised the children as citizens, but why should his behavior toward them have anything to tell us about the nature of his relationship with Neaira? In fact, as we will see presently, there can be no connection between the two, and Apollodoros is making a slippery argument.

In the Athens of Neaira's day the status of the children of a union reflected the nature of that union. If an Athenian happened to be curious about his neighbor's relationship with the woman he was living with—whether they were legally married or were less formally attached to one another—it would make sense for him to take his cues from the way the couple's children, if any, were treated. If they were raised as Athenians, the boys introduced to their father's deme, for example, then the parents were, or were pretending to be, legally married.[6]

Apollodoros claims, then, that Stephanos' behavior toward the children is compelling evidence that he was living in a faux-marital relationship with Neaira: "The sons of this Neaira, having been introduced to the phratry by Stephanos, and the daughter, having been given in marriage to an Athenian man, show very clearly that Stephanos keeps this woman as a wife" (§118). A little later in his speech, Apollodoros explains his argument further: "For this is what living together as man and wife means—to have children and introduce sons to the members of your phratry and deme, and to give your daughters, as being your own offspring, to husbands" (§122). For an Athenian man to raise his children as citizens, in other words, is evidence that his relationship with the children's mother constitutes a legal marriage. Therefore, Apollodoros argues, Stephanos' behavior toward the children implies that he has been living with Neaira in a marriage relationship.[7]

Apollodoros' argument may sound cogent, particularly if one is following it at the speed of speech, as the jurors at Neaira's trial were. Yet there is something wrong with it: the argument only works if the children in question were born from Stephanos' union with Neaira. If they were Neaira's by one or more men other than Stephanos, then Stephanos' introduction of the boys into his deme and so on would have been illegal, but it would not reflect the nature of his relationship with the boys' mother. On the other hand, if the children were Stephanos' by a citizen wife, as the defense evidently intended to argue (§119), then the fact that Stephanos raised them as citizens is unproblematic and irrelevant to the question of his relationship with Neaira. Apollodoros' use of this proof—determining the relationship between Stephanos and Neaira by the treatment of the children—is not valid unless the children were Stephanos' by Neaira.[8]

We have seen already that Apollodoros introduces the children in the early sections of his speech (§§38 and 51; cf. §13) as Neaira's brood, born before she had even met Stephanos. That Apollodoros is claiming they were Neaira's is clear enough in these passages, but the prosecutor confuses the issue later on when he is making his argument about the relationship between Stephanos and Neaira. Apollodoros suggests, subtly, that the children were born from that union: "And if it appeared . . . that Stephanos here had married a citizen woman and that these children were his by another woman, the citizen, and not by Neaira, I was willing to withdraw from the case and not bring this indictment" (§121). The ambiguity should warn us that Apollodoros is trying to pull a fast one. The prosecution's reliance on slippery argumentation in making its case can remind us, too, of the considerable differences between our own legal standards and procedures and those of ancient Athens—where documentary evidence was scarce and (as we will see further in Chapter 8) where citizens cast their votes without receiving any instructions from the court and without reviewing the case in consultation with their fellow jurors.

We will consider in the next section and in subsequent chapters whether there is reason to believe that Neaira was in fact the mother of the children, and whether Stephanos had indeed broken the law by introducing them into Athens' citizen population.

PROOF OF CITIZENSHIP

The question of Phano's citizenship is connected to the larger story of her two marriages to Athenian citizens. We will be discussing those in later chapters, and will put off until then consideration of her parentage.

As for Proxenos and Ariston, the proof Apollodoros offers that they were Neaira's sons is not convincing. As we have seen,

Apollodoros introduces the boys as well as Phano into his narrative of Neaira's history when describing her move from Megara to Athens with Stephanos. He gives us an account of a private conversation he alleges took place between Stephanos and Neaira not long before their move: "Stephanos, encouraging her in Megara with his words and bragging that Phrynion would pay if he laid a hand on her, said that he would keep Neaira as a wife, and he would introduce the sons she had at the time to the members of his phratry as if they were his own, and he would make them citizens, and no one would harm her. He came here from Megara with her and with the three children, Proxenos and Ariston and a daughter whom they now call Phano" (§38).[9]

To those of us who have time to study the speech—unlike the jurors trying the case, who had to assimilate the information the prosecution was feeding them in "real time"—it is obvious that Apollodoros cannot have known what Stephanos told Neaira in a private conversation in Megara more than twenty-five years before. Clearly, he is injecting into a fabricated conversation exactly what he wants the jurors to think Stephanos' intentions were. But the assertion that Proxenos and Ariston were Neaira's sons, inserted here into a dramatic framework, may not have struck the majority of the jurors as incredible given that they did not have time to dwell on the statement's veracity. The prosecution has adopted a rhetorically effective strategy for introducing the question of the children to the jury: simply asserting as uncontested fact what it wants the jury to believe.

Much of Apollodoros' speech is concerned with detailing the alleged misdeeds of Phano. We hear comparatively little about Proxenos and Ariston, but Apollodoros does finally address the question of their parentage toward the end of his speech. He is attempting to diminish the force of an argument he anticipates Stephanos will make when he speaks in Neaira's

defense: "I hear that Stephanos is going to make some such defense as this, that he does not keep Neaira as his wife, but as a
hetaira, and that the children are not hers, but were born to him
from another woman, a citizen whom he will say he married at
an earlier date, a relative of his" (§119).

The dispute about the parentage of the boys—whether they
were indeed Neaira's and not born to Stephanos by a citizen
wife—might have been resolved in minutes if the Athenians
had been in a position to fingerprint newborns and issue them
with birth certificates. As it was, the state did not keep records
on the births and deaths of the polis' inhabitants. This meant
that in order to prove one's parentage one had to rely on the
evidence of witnesses—friends and relatives of the family who
had been present, for example, at the child's *amphidromia,* a ceremony performed within ten days of a baby's birth during which
the child was named and publicly recognized as legitimate by
its father. Membership in a phratry or deme—which would also
be corroborated by witnesses—likewise constituted good evidence of legitimacy, since care was taken by the members of
those associations to ensure that a candidate was qualified by
birth for enrollment.[10]

Apollodoros, of course, needed to prove the negative, that
Proxenos and Ariston were *not* legitimate. He could hardly collect a posse of Athenian citizens who were ready to testify that
they had not attended one or the other's amphidromia. And
making matters far worse, Proxenos and Ariston *had,* by the
prosecution's own admission, been enrolled in Stephanos' phratry and deme.

There was very little that Apollodoros could offer as proof
of his contention that the boys were Neaira's children, and yet
it was necessary for him to attempt to undermine the argument
he thought Stephanos was going to make. After telling the jury
what he expects his opponent will say, therefore, Apollodoros
characterizes the words he has put in Stephanos' mouth as a

shameless argument, and he accuses Stephanos of having induced witnesses to provide false testimony in the case: Apollodoros tells us that he has had to respond "to the shamelessness of Stephanos' argument and of those suborned by him to give evidence" (§120). But apart from this slander and negative spin, Apollodoros has only one dart in his quiver, and the most substantial piece of evidence he can offer against the legitimacy of Proxenos and Ariston is, as we will see, not convincing.

JUDICIAL TORTURE

Except in a few exceptional circumstances, Athens' slaves could not give evidence in court unless it was extracted under torture, a method of inquisition thought by some to yield the most accurate information. "You consider the torture of slaves in both private and public matters to be the most accurate of all proofs," Demosthenes writes in his speech *Against Onetor I*. He continues: "And whenever slaves and free men are both available, and information has to be obtained, you don't use the evidence of the free men, but you torture the slaves and seek in that way to find the truth. Reasonably too, gentlemen of the jury. For some of those who have given testimony in the past have been shown not to be telling the truth. But none of those who have been tortured have ever been refuted, shown to have said things as a result of the torture that were not true." Extolling the value of information obtained through the torture of slaves happens to have been to the advantage of the speaker in this case. We will see in a moment that litigants for whom this was not true expressed quite contrary opinions about the value of slave testimony.[11]

Slaves, then, could be required to give evidence under torture, but those from whom testimony was desired could be subjected to the examination only if both parties to a dispute consented to it. The litigant interested in obtaining the testimony would issue a challenge, either offering to hand over his own slaves for torture or demanding that his opponent do the same. If the litigants reached an agreement about the challenge and its terms—how the torture was to be administered, for example, and what consequences would result from the procedure—the slaves whose testimony was at issue would be tortured in public, though not inside the courtroom, either by the litigants themselves or by an official torturer. At the same time they would be required to respond to a series of prepared questions.[12]

In his comic play *Frogs*, Aristophanes parodies an arrangement made by disputants to examine a slave under torture. The characters Aiakos and Xanthias—the latter has been accused of stealing a dog (specifically Cerberus, the three-headed guard dog of Hades)—decide to resolve their dispute by extracting testimony from the purported slave Dionysos. The two quickly come to a series of agreements about the procedure. They discuss the type of torture that will be inflicted on Dionysos, where it will be administered, the consequences of the procedure for Xanthias, and whether remuneration will be paid in the event that Dionysos is maimed:

> XANTHIAS: By Zeus, if I ever came here before I wish to be dead, or if I stole something of yours worth even one hair. But I will make you a very noble offer: take this slave here and torture him. If you ever catch me in wrongdoing, take me and kill me.
> AIAKOS: And how am I to torture him?
> XANTHIAS: Every way you can. Tie him to a ladder, hang him up, whip him with a bristling lash, flay him, stretch him, pour vinegar in his nostrils, put bricks on top of him, and everything else—except don't beat him with a leek or a young onion.
> AIAKOS: What you say is reasonable. And if I maim

your slave when I beat him, money will be put on
deposit for you to cover the damages.

XANTHIAS: Don't bother. Just take him off and beat
him.

AIAKOS: I'll do it here rather, so he can talk in front
of you.

The principal joke of the passage is that Dionysos is a god who
has exchanged clothing with his slave Xanthias and is now having a hard time proving it. (Greek gods, it would seem, had as
much trouble establishing their credentials as Athenian citizens
had.) Xanthias, in turn, is taking full advantage of his temporarily elevated position.[13]

In Aristophanes' scene, Aiakos is quite willing to see Dionysos beaten, but had he not been he could have refused Xanthias' offer to surrender his "slave." In the real world of Athenian law, the party to whom a challenge for torture was issued
was not obligated to accept it, and very often litigants refused
to do so. We see an instance of such a refusal, and at the same
time a further affirmation of the value of examination under
torture, in Lysias' speech *On the Olive Stump*. Lysias' client stood
accused of uprooting from his land the stump of a sacred olive
tree, one of a number of trees, owned by the state, that were
thought to have sprung from the olive shoot the goddess Athena
planted on the Acropolis in Athens' mythological past. The offense may seem trivial to us, but Lysias' client faced a serious
penalty: exile, at the least, and perhaps execution. He had hoped
in his defense to offer the testimony of his own slaves, but the
prosecutor refused his challenge:[14]

I went to him [the prosecutor], taking witnesses with
me, and I said that I still had all the slaves I had owned
when I took over the land, and I was ready, if he
wanted, to offer them for torture. I thought that this

would be a very strong test of what he was saying and of my actions. But he declined, saying that one cannot trust servants. Now, it seems extraordinary to me that slaves—who accuse *themselves* under torture, when they know very well that they are going to be put to death—would prefer to endure torture rather than to denounce their masters, for whom they naturally bear the utmost hostility, and thereby put an end to their suffering.[15]

Apollodoros had no more luck than Lysias' client. He challenged Stephanos to surrender four slaves for examination under torture: Thratta and Kokkaline, whom Neaira had taken with her when she left Phrynion's house for Megara roughly thirty years before, and Xennis and Drosis, slaves Neaira had purchased while living in Athens with Stephanos. These women would be in a better position than anyone, Apollodoros figured, to provide evidence about the parentage of the children (§§120–121). According to the terms he proposed, if Stephanos accepted the challenge, the outcome of the prosecution's charge against Neaira would rest on the testimony of these slaves: "And if it appeared from the examination by torture that Stephanos here had married a citizen woman and that these children were his by another woman, the citizen, and not by Neaira, I was willing to withdraw from the case and not bring this indictment" (§121). What Apollodoros does not spell out for us in this passage is the penalty that would have been imposed on Neaira and Stephanos if the slaves' testimony went against them. Probably Neaira would have been sold into slavery and the children declared aliens. At the least the children would have been rendered vulnerable to litigation challenging their status as citizens.[16]

The future of Stephanos' extended family, then, would have

been riding on the outcome of the torture of these women, whose response to the ordeal could not be anticipated: "I think you know," an alleged murderer said to a jury in the last quarter of the fifth century, "that those who are being tortured say whatever they think the ones doing most of the torturing want to hear." It is not in the least surprising, therefore, that Stephanos refused Apollodoros' challenge, preferring to lay his defense before an Athenian court. He would indeed have been a fool to hazard Neaira's freedom and the children's citizenship on the uncertainty of his slaves' response to physical abuse. It is just possible, too, that sympathy for the would-be victims played a part in the defense's decision to refuse the challenge: Thratta and Kokkaline were in their mid-forties at least at the time of the trial and may have been substantially older, and they had been in Neaira's service for at least thirty years. Some degree of affection may well have existed between the slaves and their owners.[17]

Stephanos' refusal to hand the slaves over for torture was the only evidence Apollodoros had to offer against the argument he imagined Stephanos would be making in his defense speech (that is, that the children were not Neaira's but were his by a citizen wife). In the last minutes of his own speech Apollodoros did what little he could to undermine the defense: "I issued the challenge to Stephanos here, gentlemen, and he was unwilling to accept it. Does it not seem to you, then, sirs, that a judgment has already been given by this Stephanos himself, and has he not shown that Neaira is guilty under the indictment I brought, and that I have told you the truth and introduced truthful testimony, and that everything he is going to say is a lie, and he will expose himself as saying nothing sound, since he was unwilling to surrender for torture the slave women I demanded?" (§125). Apollodoros is sounding desperate. Given what we have said about the inadvisability of Stephanos' surrendering the slaves for torture, we may conclude that the prosecution provides us with no good reason to believe that Neaira was the mother of Proxenos and Ariston.[18]

YOUR THREE SONS

Apollodoros has not only failed to substantiate his claim that Neaira was the boys' mother, but he has also provided us with a compelling reason *not* to believe him. As we have seen, Proxenos and Ariston had been introduced by Stephanos into his phratry and deme and had evidently sailed through the scrutinies that preceded enrollment in those associations. If any doubt had ever been expressed on those occasions about the boys' legitimacy, we may imagine that Apollodoros would have brought the fact to our attention.

The same argument can be used against Apollodoros' contention that Neaira was the mother also of Antidorides, a third son whom Apollodoros mentions for the first time toward the end of his speech. "These women know very well," he says, referring to the slaves he demanded for torture, "that Proxenos, now dead, Ariston, who is still alive, Antidorides the runner, and Phano, who used to be called Strybele, . . . are Neaira's" (§121). We happen to know that Stephanos' father was named Antidorides. Since Athenian boys tended to be named after their grandfathers, we can be reasonably confident that Antidorides was Stephanos' son, and we may guess that he was Stephanos' firstborn son. He may also have been Neaira's child, born to the couple after Neaira moved to Athens with Stephanos. But in that case—if Antidorides' birth indeed postdated Neaira's introduction into Stephanos' home (timing likely to have cast suspicion on the boy's parentage)—we would expect Stephanos to have met with some resistance when he presented the boy to his phratry and deme. Apollodoros, however, was unable to dredge up any residue of doubt that had attached to Antidorides' legitimacy.

Stephanos, on the other hand, evidently *was* able to find witnesses willing to testify that Antidorides, Proxenos, and Ariston were legitimate. As we have seen, Apollodoros attempts to undermine the credibility of their testimony before the fact by suggesting that Stephanos had induced his witnesses to lie on his behalf (§120). Either Stephanos is telling the truth, it seems, or Apollodoros is up against a well-rehearsed cabal of citizens willing to give false testimony to the court—a prosecutable offense. Probably Stephanos is telling the truth. Antidorides, Proxenos, and Ariston, we may believe, were his sons by a citizen wife, born prior to Neaira's move to Athens.[19]

Having unraveled Apollodoros' rhetorical strategy as far as the parentage of the male children is concerned, we can return to his narrative of Neaira's history where we left off. Stephanos decided in Megara to take Neaira back with him to Athens. He promised to be a kind of savior to her: he would protect her from Phrynion, and he intended to introduce her sons illegally into the citizen population. So much we are told by the prosecution. But the conversation Apollodoros reproduces, in which these promises were allegedly made, almost certainly never took place, and Neaira very probably was not the mother of Proxenos and Ariston.

IV

STEPHANOS,

BREADWINNER

AND

CHAMPION

According to Apollodoros, Neaira had much to gain from a relationship with Stephanos—residency in Athens, a measure of protection from Phrynion, and the perquisites of citizenship for her sons. There is reason to doubt that she was in fact the mother of the boys in question, but as we will see later in this chapter, Phrynion *did* pose a real threat to the new couple. Presumably Neaira was eager for the security that a stable relationship with a man could offer.

Stephanos had reasons of his own for bringing Neaira home with him. One explanation for his decision was probably the obvious one: Neaira was an attractive woman whose peculiar training made her a desirable companion. If, as we have suggested, Stephanos was also the father of two or three boys at this time, he may have seen Neaira as a potential helpmate in raising them. (The citizen wife who he claimed was their mother seems no longer to have been in the picture. Probably she had died.) It may be, finally, that genuine affection had built up between Stephanos and Neaira during his stay in Megara.

Apollodoros attributes to Stephanos a baser motivation for installing Neaira in his home: "There were two reasons why he came with her to Athens, so that he would have a beautiful hetaira free of charge, and so that she would earn money for the things they needed and would support the household. For he had no income except whatever he got from being a sycophant" (§39). We can hardly quibble with the first of Apollodoros' reasons, of course, but we should look more closely at the prosecutor's second claim, that Stephanos was motivated by penury and intended to support the household by prostituting Neaira. Had she indeed moved back to Athens only to find herself again sexually exploited, this time compelled to support her lover and the children as well as herself? What kind of a man had Neaira attached herself to?

PLAYING THE SYCOPHANT

Let us consider first whether Apollodoros is telling the truth about Stephanos' financial situation and means of support. Apollodoros tells us that at this stage of his life Stephanos was relatively poor. In support of this contention he discusses and puts a value on the house into which Stephanos moved Neaira: "Stephanos brought Neaira and the children into the little house that he had near the Whispering Hermes [a statue whose location is unknown], between the houses of Dorotheos of Eleusis and Kleinomachos. Spintharos has now bought the place from him for seven minai [700 drachmas]" (§39). Now, house prices in the fourth century seem to have ranged between 300 and 12,000 drachmas, so Apollodoros, if his information about the sale price is correct, is right to point out that Stephanos' cottage was worth comparatively little. Stephanos' neighbor Dorotheos, however, is known to have been a man of some property: in 366 and 357 he served as trierarch—the captain and financier of an Athenian warship—a responsibility which only the wealthiest citizens undertook. This does not prove much: Stephanos' modest home may have sat in the midst of far more expensive houses, or Dorotheos' home may not have been ostentatious. But it does suggest that the neighborhood in which Stephanos and Neaira lived was not so undesirable as to preclude the residence there of wealthy men.[1]

Apollodoros tells us, further, that Stephanos' little house was his only property: "This was the property Stephanos had and nothing else besides" (§39). But he does not offer any proof for the claim, such as witnesses who could give evidence about Stephanos' situation. Fifteen years or more later Stephanos evidently owned land in the country (§65). It is possible that this property was in his possession already in 371, when he brought Neaira home with him. In the mid-350s, too, Stephanos was able to marry Phano off with a dowry of 3,000 drachmas (§50)—more than four times the value of the house he moved Neaira into—which suggests that his estate at *that* time, at least, was far more substantial than Apollodoros suggests it was in the 370s. Apollodoros, then, may be telling us the truth about Stephanos' assets, but there is no compelling evidence that substantiates his remarks.[2]

Apollodoros claims, second, that Stephanos "had no income except whatever he got from being a sycophant." This statement requires explanation, because the term "sycophant" in the context of Athenian law has nothing to do with the word's modern meaning, although in both cases the term is insulting. Sycophancy was a charge litigants regularly leveled against their opponents in court, whether there was any truth to the accusation or not. In calling Stephanos a sycophant, Apollodoros means that his opponent used to make money by exploiting his right as an Athenian citizen to participate in the assembly and to bring accusations in court.

A large number of activities fell under the rubric of sycophancy. For example, because there was some danger attached to proposing a decree in the assembly—a proposer could be indicted if the decree he backed conflicted with standing statutes—the citizen who wanted a decree proposed might hire a third party (the sycophant) to make the proposal under his own name. (We will see an example of this in Chapter 7.) Similarly, an Athenian who wished to prosecute someone might hire a third party to bring the case, either to avoid the penalties that were sometimes imposed on unsuccessful prosecutors, or because the man doing the hiring was himself not an accomplished speaker. (Litigants in Athenian courts were not represented by counsel but had to address the court themselves.)[3]

But there are other less savory means by which sycophants might profit. There were certain legal procedures, for example, in which successful prosecutors received a portion of the fines paid by defendants. The reward was intended to encourage would-be prosecutors to come forward, since the Athenian legal system depended on voluntarism. But it also left the door open for abuse: sycophants exploited the system by habitually bringing charges, sometimes ill-founded, in the hope of profiting from a victory in court. Alternatively, and more despicably, sycophants might blackmail would-be defendants, threatening to bring charges unless their victims paid them off. Even innocent men might sometimes prefer to pay off a blackmailer rather than submit to the bother and risk of a jury trial.[4]

Shortly after making his initial charge of sycophancy, Apollodoros provides a bit of detail about the sorts of activities he claims Stephanos was involved in at the time he began his relationship with Neaira: "Stephanos here was not yet earning anything worth mentioning from his political activity. For he was not yet a public speaker, but still a sycophant—one of those who stand near the speaker's platform and shout, and who bring indictments and denunciations for money, and who affix their names to other people's motions—until he came under the influence of Kallistratos of the deme Aphidna" (§43). The charges Apollodoros makes here are vague and, taken by themselves, unconvincing. But other details in Apollodoros' account suggest that Stephanos was not above profiting from sycophantic litigation.

Apollodoros tells us that Stephanos was a sycophant until he hooked up with Kallistratos, a prominent political figure of the day. Afterward, it is implied, Stephanos took a higher road, involving himself in more traditional political activities. Although we have only Apollodoros' word for it, it is likely that Stephanos was indeed associated with Kallistratos. We know, at least, that Stephanos brought charges against a certain Xenokleides, a poet, in 369, not long after Xenokleides had opposed Kallistratos in the assembly. The prosecution was successful, and Xenokleides was disfranchised as a result. Apollodoros mentions the case in connection with his account of Neaira's years in Nikarete's brothel, since he claims that Xenokleides was one of Neaira's lovers at that time. (This is a delicious coincidence, if true, but Xenokleides may have claimed as much only in order to taunt the man responsible for his disfranchisement.)

> After this, then, she was working openly in Corinth and was well known. In addition to her other lovers she had Xenokleides the poet and Hipparchos the actor, and they paid for her and had her. I cannot present you with the testimony of Xenokleides to show you I'm telling the truth, since the laws don't allow him to give evidence. When you were sending aid to the Spartans, having

been persuaded to do so by Kallistratos, Xenokleides addressed the assembly, speaking in opposition to sending the help. . . . [H]e was exempt by law [because of certain tax-collecting responsibilities] and did not go out on that expedition, but he was indicted by Stephanos here for failure to serve. He was slandered in the court and was convicted and disfranchised. (§§26–27)

Since Xenokleides could no longer speak in the assembly or lawcourts as a result of the trial, Stephanos' prosecution had effectively rid Kallistratos of a political opponent. We may believe either that Kallistratos had benefited unexpectedly from Stephanos' timely prosecution, and there was no connection between the two men, or that Kallistratos had in fact orchestrated the attack and had compensated Stephanos for his role in bringing the charge. On the face of it, the latter scenario seems the more likely.[5]

We are told by Apollodoros of two other lawsuits that Stephanos is likely to have been paid for initiating. In both cases Apollodoros himself was the defendant. We will discuss these cases in further detail in Chapter 7, when we consider the legal antecedents to the present trial.

Stephanos, then, probably had engaged in sycophantic activity in his career, though whether he did so habitually, as Apollodoros would have us believe, is anyone's guess. His willingness to sell his civic rights at a price, however, does not imply a similarly cavalier attitude toward the person of his lover. We will consider next whether Neaira did in fact continue prostituting herself while she lived with Stephanos, and whether he went so far as to act as her pimp.

THE VERSATILE RADISH

Apollodoros paints a fairly ugly picture of the goings-on in Stephanos' little house: "[S]he kept working as much as before when she was with him, but she demanded more money from those who wanted to have sex with her, on the pretext that she was now someone's wife and was living with a husband. And Stephanos teamed up with her in blackmail: if he came upon some wealthy, inexperienced foreigner who was a lover of hers, he would lock up the man indoors and exact a lot of money from him, as being a *moichos*" (§41). The term moichos is very often translated as "adulterer" and *moicheia* as "adultery," but the meanings of the words do not correspond precisely. A moichos committed moicheia when he had sex with a free woman who was the dependent of some man—not just the man's wife, then, but his daughter or sister, mother, niece, or concubine, if they were under his legal protection. According to Apollodoros, Stephanos made a habit of finding Neaira in bed with gullible foreigners, after which intrusion he pretended outrage and kept the man in custody until the victim paid or made arrangements to pay ransom.[6]

Now, *if* Stephanos in fact did this—and if Neaira had not been prostituting herself when he did—he would actually have been acting within his rights. Imprisoning a moichos caught in flagrante delicto with a female dependent was one of several options available to an Athenian man who burst in on such a scene. The aggrieved male could also bring the offender to court, or he could kill the moichos with impunity—if not without some risk: the killing rendered the killer vulnerable to prosecution, but if he could prove that he had executed a moichos caught in the act, he would escape punishment. Lysias' speech *On the Murder of Eratosthenes*, which we mentioned already in Chapter 1, concerns Euphiletos' execution of a man he found in bed with his wife. As Euphiletos tells it, Eratosthenes offered to pay ransom, but the speaker was intent on killing him instead. Before dispatching his wife's lover, however, Euphiletos gave him a bit of a talking-to, his victim tied up at this point and still naked: "*I* will not be killing you," he said, "but rather the law of our polis will, which you transgressed and considered of less account than your pleasures." It is a melodramatic sendoff for a man who, Euphiletos tells us elsewhere, made an art of debauching women.[7]

There was another option available for aggrieved males as well: physical abuse. This could presumably take the form of beatings or whippings imposed on the moichos, but men interested in obtaining redress for the violation of their womenfolk were by no means limited to the mundane. Their abuse could involve quite ingenious forms of torture meant to humiliate the violator. In his comic play *Clouds*, in a conversation between the characters Unjust Discourse and Just Discourse, Aristophanes refers to two penalties that were evidently famous for being imposed on at least some unlucky *moichoi*, the insertion of a radish into the offender's anus, and the depilation of his pubic area using hot ash:

UNJUST DISCOURSE: If you chance to be caught as a
moichos, you will say to the husband that you have
done nothing wrong; then cite the example of Zeus,
that even *he* cannot resist love and women. How
could you, who are mortal, be stronger than a god?
JUST DISCOURSE: What if he follows your advice and is
radished and plucked with hot ash? What will he be
able to say to keep from having his asshole enlarged?
UNJUST DISCOURSE: And if he becomes wide-assed,
where's the harm?
JUST DISCOURSE: Whatever could be worse than that?!
(1079–1085)

As punishment for his offense, that is, the moichos could be subjected to a forcible feminization, penetrated anally by a root vegetable and depilated about his genitals as a woman might be. The radish that the aggrieved party could choose to wield, by the way, was probably not the dainty red salad component one finds nowadays in the produce aisle, but rather a much larger variety of the vegetable—an instrument of sufficient proportions for a cuckolded husband to effectively register his displeasure. (As one scholar writes, "what is envisaged is surrogate buggery using a vegetable of a size suitable to ensure that forced penetration would be both possible and painful.") Considering the dangers faced by libidinous moichoi, we may wonder, with the comic poet Xenarchos, "How, mistress Aphrodite of the sea, do they ever manage to fuck married women when, while making their move, they remember the laws of Draco?"[8]

It is worth noting here that some scholars have supposed that the cuckolds of Athens were wont to insert into the rectums of moichoi not only radishes, but fish, and not just any fish, but the scorpion fish, "an unimpressive inhabitant of the Mediterranean in size (around 25 cm long, 5 × 3 cm thick) and shape, but equipped with severely poisonous spines." One scholar successfully refutes this suggestion, in part by describing in detail precisely how awful a punishment penetration by scorpion fish would be:

Supposing that it could be used, the size, shape, and slippery surface of the scorpion fish would ensure that penetration is not particularly difficult. But removing it would be almost impossible without major surgery. If one tried to slip it out, the spines would be pulled up and hooked into the internal walls of the rectum, causing severe injury, and eventually ripping the rectum apart, or even breaking inside. Simultaneously the poison would spread causing swelling and making the whole undertaking almost impossible, while the pain would be excruciating. Even if a skilful medic removed it successfully the poison in the large intestine, the possible presence of fragments from the spines, the swelling and the injuries, combined with the limited assistance

which contemporary medicine could offer, might prove
lethal.

An Athenian court may have condoned a man's execution of
a moichos in the heat of the moment, but inflicting "sadistic,
potentially lethal tortures" was not in keeping with the Athenian way of thinking or with the intentions of the law that gov-
erned the treatment of moichoi.[9]

Stephanos, of course, however many gruesome alternatives
were available to him, was more interested in filthy lucre than
in poetic justice—or so Apollodoros tells us—for as we have
seen, he allegedly made a habit of barging in on Neaira's foreign
lovers and extorting money from them. Can we believe Apollodoros' story? Like so much of what we are told in this speech, we
simply cannot know what the truth was. Apollodoros' version of
what happened is certainly not impossible. The scam he has in
mind—trapping and exacting money from unwitting moichoi—
was evidently a common enough trick in the arsenal of Athens'
con men. On the other hand, Apollodoros is eager to blacken
Stephanos' reputation as much as he can in his speech, because
his object in proceeding against Neaira is to penalize her lover.
And Apollodoros offers no proof whatever that Stephanos and
Neaira were ever involved in such a scheme. He evidently had
not persuaded any of these numerous defrauded foreigners
whose existence he knew of to give testimony at Neaira's trial.
Or perhaps there were no such aggrieved foreigners to be
found.[10]

Apollodoros also does not offer any testimony to support
his claim that Neaira continued to work as a prostitute after she
moved to Athens with Stephanos. We did see in Chapter 1 that
the comic poet Philetairos makes a joke in his play *Huntress*
about Neaira and a number of other women prostituting themselves at an advanced age: Neaira was among those who "rotted
away" fucking. The play has been dated between 370 and 365,

and if this is right, it was performed not very many years after Neaira moved in with Stephanos. It may be that Neaira prostituted herself in those early years, and that Philetairos is referring in his play to relatively recent behavior on her part. But there is no need to interpret the passage so closely. It is a joke, after all, and is not necessarily steeped in historical accuracy. Philetairos can as easily be referring to Neaira's pre-Stephanic sex life, the years she spent selling her body in Megara before he brought her to Athens. Besides, if Philetairos can refer to Neaira as "rotting away" at the age of thirty-five—the oldest she is likely to have been in 365—then chances are he would have said the same about her were he referring to her sex life in 371, the year she left Megara for Athens, when she was at most twenty-nine. Either way, she was past her prime.[11]

We need not believe that the couple ran their home like a brothel. They may just as well have lived a relatively normal life—two unmarried adults, one a former prostitute, raising four children together in what passed as a family unit, their days whiled away in a modest home somewhere in Attica.

But even ordinary households host their share of family dramas.

RECONCILIATION

Phrynion burst back into Neaira's life soon after she set up housekeeping with Stephanos. Apollodoros tells us that when Phrynion heard she was back in town and found out where she was living, he got some young men together and went to Stephanos' house to try to drag her away with him (§40). In doing this, Phrynion was acting the part of a master who was asserting his legal claim to a runaway slave. A slave owner's first step in claiming that someone was his property was to hale that person into slavery in just this way.[12]

Phrynion may in fact have had a legitimate claim to Neaira:

she does not seem to have ever paid back the money he lent her when she bought her freedom from Timanoridas and Eukrates in Corinth. We do not know precisely what arrangement was made between them at that time, but it is possible that Neaira's failure to repay the loan had rendered her vulnerable to reenslavement. For two reasons, however, this is unlikely. If Phrynion's claim to Neaira were a strong one, Apollodoros would surely have made a point of telling the jurors that she was in effect Phrynion's slave when she moved to Athens with Stephanos. Apollodoros, however, says nothing of the kind in his account of Phrynion's seizure of Neaira and the arbitration procedure the incident led to. Further, if Phrynion indeed had a right to claim Neaira as his slave, it is very unlikely that she would have returned to Athens at all, whatever the conditions in Megara, and however secure she felt in Stephanos' arms.

In claiming Neaira as his slave, Phrynion was perhaps hoping that Stephanos would not take the legal steps necessary to defend her, or hoping that if Stephanos *did* oppose him Neaira would be unable to provide sufficient proof of her status. He may, too, have been acting merely from an irrational vindictiveness, still wounded because Neaira had fled from him two or three years earlier, taking some of his property with her when she went.

Whatever Phrynion's expectations, Stephanos came through splendidly for Neaira. In response to Phrynion's action, Stephanos took the appropriate legal step of asserting Neaira's status as a freedwoman. The issue then became a matter for the law to decide. Phrynion brought an action against Stephanos— the natural next step in the progression of the affair—which would, when brought to court, have resulted in a jury's determination of Neaira's status, slave or free. Stephanos was required together with two other men, who must have been his friends, to stand surety for Neaira while the case was pending (§40). That is, Stephanos and his friends acted as guarantors that

Neaira would remain in Athens for the trial. This was standard procedure when one of the parties to a lawsuit was a metic, since aliens were naturally perceived as posing a greater flight risk than Athenian citizens. If Neaira had failed to appear for trial, Stephanos and the others standing surety would presumably have been compelled to compensate Phrynion for his loss of property, perhaps in this case a sum equal to the amount he had lent Neaira in Corinth.[13]

The case, however, never went to court. The parties to the dispute decided to settle the matter by submitting it to private arbitration. There were public arbitrators in Athens before whom certain types of cases were necessarily brought during their preliminary stages. (Indeed, all Athenian males were required to serve as public arbitrators for one year, when they turned sixty and were no longer liable for military service.) But the arbitration to which Stephanos and Phrynion submitted was a procedure they undertook voluntarily, and the arbitrators deciding the issue would be friends of the disputants rather than appointees of the state. Stephanos and Phrynion agreed to be bound by the decision of the arbitrators. There would be no appeal to a court after the fact, as there could be after a public procedure.[14]

Phrynion and Stephanos selected three arbitrators, one to represent each side to the dispute and a third who was agreeable to both parties (§45). They met together in a temple—private arbitrations were regularly conducted in public places—and after hearing evidence from both sides, the arbitrators arrived at a solution. Neither party can be said to have won the case. Private arbitration characteristically resulted in a compromise meant to satisfy all concerned parties while giving a definitive victory to no one. And so we find here a solution, bizarre, perhaps, to modern eyes, from which Phrynion and Stephanos could each take some satisfaction:

They got together in the temple, and the arbitrators heard about what had happened from both sides and from the woman herself. Then they gave their opinion, and these men abided by it: the woman was free and was her own mistress; she was to return to Phrynion everything she had taken from him except for her clothing and jewelry and maidservants, which had been purchased for her; and she was to live with each of the men for equal periods in alternation. But if the disputants should arrive between them at another agreement, that agreement was to be valid. The man who had her at any particular time was to provide for the woman's maintenance, and the disputants were thereafter to be on good terms with one another and were not to bear one another ill will. (§46)[15]

The arbitrators had established that Neaira was a freedwoman and not Phrynion's slave. This was a clear win for our heroine, but for all her theoretical freedom Neaira was not much better off than she had been in her days as Timanoridas' and Eukrates' sex slave. In a very real sense she remained in the power of the men in her life, who disposed of her body as they saw fit.

There were, quite possibly, no further problems between Stephanos and Phrynion. They did evidently take turns at enjoying Neaira's company, at least for a time. Apollodoros tells us that after Stephanos and Phrynion had reconciled, they and the men who had taken part in the arbitration procedure met from time to time at the house of whichever of the two men Neaira was staying with. Apollodoros further reports—and he offers witnesses to corroborate the story—that "Neaira ate and drank with them as a hetaira would" on these occasions (§48). We would, I think, expect nothing less.

We hear nothing further about the titillating agreement that resulted from the arbitration procedure, and Apollodoros never mentions Phrynion again in his speech. Indeed, we have no further information from any source about Phrynion's subsequent activities. It seems clear that he was no longer in the picture by the time of Neaira's trial. Perhaps he had died, or perhaps he and Stephanos had come to an agreement at some point which, whatever its particulars, allowed Neaira and Stephanos to enjoy at last a kind of monogamy.

V

PHANO'S
FIRST
MARRIAGE

A dozen years or more after Neaira's body was used as a bargaining chip at that arbitration hearing, Phano—whom Apollodoros, as we have seen, claims was Neaira's daughter—was married off by Stephanos to an Athenian citizen, Phrastor of the deme Aigilia (fig. 10).[1]

AN IMPERFECT MARRIAGE

We know nothing about Phano's new husband other than what we are told in the speech against Neaira. Apollodoros says that

FIGURE 10. A newlywed couple travels to the groom's house on a
mule cart. The Metropolitan Museum of Art, Purchase,
Walter C. Baker Gift, 1956 (56.11.1).

Phrastor was "a hard worker, who had amassed his property through careful living" (§50)—a pitchfork-wielding American Gothic kind of fellow, we are to imagine, who had now crossed paths with the debauched daughter of a debauchee.

Phrastor may not have been as old as Grant Wood's dour farmer, but he was almost certainly older than Phano. Although women married usually in their teens, shortly after puberty, men married for the first time more often in their thirties. (It was desirable that girls marry at a young age for a number of reasons, among them that women were supposed to be virgins at the time of their marriage and were thought to be by nature more lustful than men: not for nothing did Tiresias, the legendary seer, report that women enjoy sex nine times more than men do.) We do not know whether Phrastor's marriage to Phano was his first, though we are told that he did not yet have any legitimate children (§55). Probably, then, he was in his thirties or forties, fifteen to twenty years older than Phano, and old enough to have settled irreversibly into the frugal way of life to which his new wife, we are told, found it difficult to adapt: "When she went to Phrastor's house . . . she did not know how to conform to his habits, but she pursued her mother's lifestyle and the licentiousness of that house, since, I suppose, she was brought up in that way" (§50).[2]

Clearly, at least as far as we can tell from Apollodoros' account, Phano and her husband were incompatible, and that fact was not lost on Phrastor. Phano fell far short of being the obedient, submissive wife he had been in the market for—though the fact that Apollodoros does *not* tell us that she had had other men before her marriage or that she did so while married suggests that she was not the wanton he would have us believe. Probably she was faithful to Phrastor, and the chances are good that she had been a virgin when she married. But because of their incompatibility, principally, Phrastor threw Phano out of the house, which is to say that he divorced her: a woman's move from her husband's home—whether at his insistence or of her own volition—was all that was required legally for a divorce to have occurred. They had been married for about a year when he divorced her, and Phano was pregnant by that time with Phrastor's son.[3]

Apollodoros tells us that there was a second reason for Phrastor's disenchantment with his wife: he had discovered that she was in fact Neaira's daughter and not Stephanos' by a citizen wife, as Stephanos had led him to believe. Phano, in other words, was allegedly not an Athenian, and could not produce citizen offspring, and Stephanos had broken the law by giving Phano in marriage to Phrastor:

> Phrastor saw that she was not well-behaved and that she was unwilling to obey him. At the same time, he had learned by then without a doubt that she was not Stephanos' daughter, but Neaira's. He realized that he had been deceived when he married her, taking her on the understanding that she was the daughter of Stephanos and not Neaira and that she had been born to Stephanos by a citizen wife before he lived with Neaira. Phrastor was angry because of all of this, and he felt that he had been treated outrageously and deceived. He threw her out of the house when she was already pregnant, after living with her for about a year, and he did not give back her dowry. (§51)

Apollodoros, it will be remembered, was seeking to prove to the jurors both that Neaira was an alien and that Stephanos was living with her as his wife. His account of Phano's relationship with Phrastor is the first of three stories he tells about the girl that are meant to support the prosecution's case in two ways: first, by showing that Stephanos and others made it clear by their actions that Phano was an alien rather than a citizen, which itself implies that Phano's mother—Neaira, allegedly—

was an alien; and second (only ostensibly a contradiction of the first), by showing that Stephanos treated Phano as a citizen, which is intended as proof that Stephanos was living with Phano's mother as his wife.

It is certainly true that Stephanos treated Phano as a citizen when he gave her in marriage to an Athenian. But as we saw already in Chapter 3, this can tell us something about Stephanos' relationship with Neaira only if Phano were their daughter. Apollodoros, however, takes only a weak stab in his speech at suggesting that Phano and the boys were born to Stephanos by Neaira. For the most part he is content with attempting to prove that Neaira was their mother, whoever their father or fathers may have been, and that they were consequently not legitimate citizens. Convincing the jury of these two points would not prove that Neaira had been living in a marriage relationship with Stephanos, but it might be enough to win the prosecution a guilty verdict nonetheless. If Apollodoros could show that Stephanos had introduced noncitizens into the citizen population, the jurors might not notice that he had failed to prove his case against Neaira, or they might not care, electing to punish Stephanos by condemning Neaira on this unrelated charge.

For our present purpose, Apollodoros' slippery argumentation and its success or failure is less interesting than establishing the bare facts of Neaira's life. *Was* she in fact Phano's mother? And did Stephanos indeed break the law when he married Phano off to Athenian citizens? We will consider Apollodoros' three stories—his accounts of Phano's relations with Phrastor, Epainetos, and Theogenes—with these questions in mind.

The story of Phrastor's divorce—and Phrastor himself provided testimony in support of at least some of Apollodoros' account at Neaira's trial—appears to provide strong evidence that Phano was in fact Neaira's daughter. Phrastor had, after all, allegedly learned about his wife's parentage "without a doubt," and he was sufficiently incensed by Stephanos' deception that he kicked Phano out of his house. Apollodoros, however, does not tell us anything about Phrastor's sources of information. We are left with only his and Phrastor's word for it that Phano was Neaira's daughter and that the question of her parentage was a factor in Phrastor's divorcing her. Apollodoros, of course, has reason to lie about the matter. But Phrastor, as we shall see, may bear the ultimate responsibility for the fact that Phano's citizenship had ever been questioned. He may, that is, have made up the story about her parentage himself.

SUIT AND COUNTERSUIT

When Phano married Phrastor, Stephanos gave her a dowry of 3,000 drachmas (§50). There was nothing unusual about this, neither the amount, which seems to have been fairly average, nor the practice, which was standard. While there was no legal requirement that the female children in a family be dowered when they were married, it was something even the poorest families would attempt to do. A dowry not only made a girl a more attractive catch for would-be suitors, but it provided her with a degree of security as well. Although the money (or property) with which a woman was dowered was received by her husband and was managed by him during their marriage, it remained the possession of the woman. As long as a marriage lasted, this distinction was probably irrelevant. But if the relationship was dissolved, whatever the reason for the divorce, and regardless of who had initiated it, the husband was *required* to return the dowry—and if it was not returned immediately, then he was obliged to pay it back with interest (18 percent annually). This made the woman's position more secure because the requirement that the husband repay the dowry was a disincentive for him to divorce her or to mistreat her (which might prompt her to leave him), and because the money would in principle always be available to her to use as a dowry in a second marriage.[4]

Phrastor, who was unhappy with Phano because she was not sufficiently deferential to him, was evidently not a stickler himself for obeying authority. He failed to return Phano's dowry when he threw her out, having no right whatever to retain it. Phano returned to the bosom of her family at Stephanos' house, and Stephanos initiated a lawsuit against Phrastor with a view to getting the 3,000 drachmas back from him: "Stephanos initiated a suit for maintenance against Phrastor at the Odeum [a musical theater on the south slope of the Acropolis that was used also as a lawcourt], in accordance with the law which stipulates: if anyone divorces his wife, he is to pay back the dowry, and if he does not pay it back, he is to pay interest at a rate of nine obols [that is, one and a half drachmas per month for every one hundred drachmas, or 18 percent]; and the woman's guardian may sue on her behalf at the Odeum" (§52).[5]

Phrastor, then, found himself under attack. If he lost the lawsuit Stephanos had initiated, he would be required to pay 45 drachmas in interest per month on the 3,000-drachma dowry until he returned it to Phano. He could have submitted meekly to the suit and hoped that the court would find in his favor for some reason—quite unlikely if the facts of the case are as Apollodoros has described—but instead Phrastor threw a deft counterpunch. He initiated a suit against Stephanos for "having given in marriage to him, an Athenian, the daughter of a foreign woman, as if she were Stephanos' relative" (§52).[6]

Phrastor had effectively upped the ante. If Stephanos were found guilty of having married a foreigner's daughter to an Athenian citizen on the understanding that the bride was also a citizen, he would have been subject to very harsh penalties: *atimia*—that is, the loss of his civil rights and of the right to enter the agora and the temples—and the confiscation of his property, one third of which would then be given over to Phrastor as the successful prosecutor in the case. Obviously, there was a lot more to lose here than a 3,000-drachma dowry.[7]

To be successful in the suit brought by Phrastor, Stephanos would have to offer proof that Phano was indeed a citizen. We saw in Chapter 3 what kind of evidence a male could adduce in support of his status—witnesses who could testify to having been present at his amphidromia when a child, membership in his father's phratry and deme—hardly the rock-solid evidence to which one would want to entrust one's own citizenship status. Proof of a woman's status likewise rested on the testimony of witnesses. While girls were not introduced to their fathers' demes, as boys were, they were sometimes introduced to phratries, and phratry members could subsequently be called upon to testify to that effect. Otherwise, relatives could attest at the least to the woman having been accepted as a legitimate citizen throughout her life—recognized unreservedly by her father as his own child, for example, and married to a citizen male without any questions being raised at the time about her status.[8]

In about 345, around the time of Neaira's trial, a certain Euxitheos attempted to prove in court that he was a citizen. He introduced to the jurors numerous witnesses to testify to his mother's citizenship status: "My mother is Nikarete, the daughter of Damostratos of Melite. Which of her relatives will testify? First, a nephew; then, two sons of another nephew, and the son of a cousin, and the sons of Protomachos, who was my mother's first husband; also Eunikos of Cholargos, who married my sister, the daughter of Protomachos; finally the son of my sister. Further, the phratry and deme members of her relatives have testified to these things. What more could you need?" Euxitheos dragged a cavalcade of relatives and acquaintances to court to testify that his mother was a citizen. His example shows how much trouble it could be to establish one's status in a society in which documentary evidence was in short supply.[9]

If Phano was in fact the daughter of Neaira, and Stephanos

had indeed hoodwinked Phrastor into marrying her, then it would be surprising if Stephanos wanted to test her citizenship status in the crucible of an Athenian court. What witnesses could he present to the jurors, in that case, other than any he managed to coax into perjuring themselves? If, on the other hand, Phano *was* a citizen, Stephanos' daughter by a citizen wife, then her status and the status of her unborn child—not to mention the whole of Stephanos' property and his own ability to exercise his civil rights—would have been riding on the outcome of the proceedings Phrastor had initiated. Could Stephanos rally sufficient support among his relatives and acquaintances to convince a jury of Phano's citizenship?

Even if she *was* a citizen, the outcome of the test would be too uncertain, and a far easier escape from the predicament lay at hand: Stephanos settled with Phrastor out of court (§53). He gave up his right to the dowry and withdrew his suit for maintenance. Phrastor in turn dropped the charges he had brought against Stephanos. It had cost Stephanos and his family 3,000 drachmas, and they had come out the losers in Phrastor's game of chicken, but they had at least avoided the dangers inherent in a jury trial over Phano's citizenship.

But was she a citizen? The evidence so far is inconclusive, since Phrastor's actions in divorcing Phano and bringing his indictment against Stephanos are fully explicable whether Phano was Neaira's daughter or not. Phrastor may indeed have had information that proved that Phano was not a citizen, and this could have been a factor in his decision to divorce her. Alternatively, after he had illegally retained Phano's dowry, and not wanting to return it, Phrastor may have made up the story himself, alleging in retrospect that he had divorced Phano because of what he had learned about her parentage. Neaira had been in Stephanos' household long enough that the suggestion that she was in fact Phano's mother might be readily believed by strangers. It would have been easy enough for Phrastor to ignite doubts about her parentage, and rumors to that effect may, at any rate, already have been in the air. Bringing this quite serious charge against Stephanos, meanwhile, could be expected to have the effect that it had, compelling him to withdraw his indictment and to renounce his claim to the dowry. The allegation that Phano was Neaira's daughter need not have been true in order for Phrastor to use it to good effect as a weapon against his former father-in-law (or former father-figure-in-law).

DEATHBED CONSIDERATIONS

Not long after Phrastor threw Phano out of his house, he became seriously ill. While he was sick, Phano and Neaira took care of him, and during the same period Phrastor recognized the boy Phano had borne as his legitimate son, which is to say, as his son by a citizen wife. These are the bare facts of what happened. Obviously Phrastor's recognition of the baby as a citizen was inconvenient for Apollodoros, in trying to make a case against Neaira, because it implied that Phano was also a citizen. Apollodoros needed to explain away Phrastor's behavior toward the child, and in his speech he attributes the father's action to a number of factors.[10]

First, Apollodoros tells us, Phrastor did not have any other children. This meant that, in the event that he died from his illness (which seemed likely at the time), and unless he made a will bequeathing his property to one or more persons outside of his family, the assets he had worked so hard to amass would be inherited by his relatives, in accordance with the law: those on his father's side of the family stood to inherit first, according to a fixed order (brothers or half-brothers and their descendants first, then sisters or half-sisters and their descendants, etc.), and if there were none to inherit in that line, then relatives on his mother's side. The problem, according to Apollodoros, was that Phrastor hated these would-be inheritors: "There was a long-standing quarrel between him and his relatives, and anger and hatred" (§55). Phrastor most certainly did not want them inheriting from him.[11]

Dying without legitimate offspring was problematic for another, perhaps more serious reason as well. The Athenians were horrified at the prospect of allowing their family, or *oikos*—their house and the family members who lived in it—to die out. If the *kyrios* of an oikos—the man who was the head of the household—died without producing legitimate children, and he did not act to preserve the oikos by adopting a citizen male as his son, then the oikos became extinct upon his death. There would be no oikos member, in that case, to look after the ancestral tombs of the house or to provide offerings to the dead, very important considerations to the Athenian mind.[12]

In a mid-fourth-century speech by the orator Isaeus, *On the Estate of Menekles*, the unnamed speaker, whom Menekles had adopted decades before the trial, explains the reasoning behind the deceased's decision to adopt: "Menekles was considering how he might not be childless, and how there might be someone to take care of him in his old age and to bury him when he died, and after that to perform the customary rites for him." In another speech from the same period, Isaeus explains that the preservation of one's oikos is uppermost on the minds of all men on their deathbeds: "All men who are about to die give thought to their futures, how they will not leave their *oikoi* extinct, but that there will be someone who will offer sacrifices to the dead and perform the customary rites for them. And even if they die childless, they adopt a son and leave him behind." Phrastor's thinking when near death was, from what we are told, standard. Lying ill on his deathbed, and not yet having recognized Phano's baby as legitimate, he too was considering the future of his oikos, and wondering whether anyone would perform sacrifices on his behalf when he died.[13]

Phrastor, then, needed to adopt a child or recognize Phano's as legitimate before he died so that there would be someone to inherit his possessions and his oikos. But on top of these considerations, Apollodoros tells us, Phrastor was led astray while ill, persuaded to recognize the child by the ostensibly kind but in fact cunning ministrations of his nursemaids, Phano and Neaira herself:

> Beyond that [Phrastor's relationship with his relatives], he was childless, and he was beguiled while sick by the nursing of Neaira and her daughter. (For they used to go to him when he was sick and did not have anyone to take care of him, bringing what was needed for the illness and looking after him. You know yourselves, I imagine, how valuable a woman is as a nurse, when she tends to a man who is sick.) He was persuaded to take back and to recognize as his legitimate son the child whom the daughter of Neaira here gave birth to after she was divorced by Phrastor. (He threw her out when she was already pregnant, after he learned that she was the daughter not of Stephanos, but of Neaira, and he was angry at the deceit.) His reasoning was natural and sensible: he was in a bad way and there was no expectation that he would survive, and not wanting his relatives to inherit his property or himself to die childless, he recognized the boy as legitimate and took him into his home. (§§55–57)

Phrastor, then, was not only ill when he decided to recognize the boy as legitimate, but Apollodoros tells us that he was unduly influenced by Neaira and Phano, precisely the sort of conditions which were likely to make a man act unreasonably: under Athenian law, at least, childless Athenians were considered incompetent to dispose of their property by will if they were, among other possibilities, deranged by illness or persuaded to make the will by a woman. Surely Apollodoros wanted to suggest to the jurors that Phrastor's situation had to an extent deprived him of free will. He had made a decision which was understandable under the circumstances, but which he would never have made if he had not been near death.[14]

Apollodoros' explanation for Phrastor's behavior makes sense. The considerations he enumerates—Phrastor's fear that he was near death, his unwillingness to let his property pass to his relatives, his desire to maintain his oikos, and the hints allegedly whispered in his ear by Phano and Neaira while he was ill—*could* have prompted Phrastor to recognize as his legitimate son the child of a woman he *knew* to be an alien. So far, however, Apollodoros has not proved that his interpretation of Phrastor's behavior is the correct one. We will consider in the next section the two proofs he offers to convince the jury that Phrastor recognized the child only under duress, and that his recognition of the boy does *not* mean he was in fact persuaded that the boy's mother was an Athenian citizen.

SWEARING AT THE ARBITRATOR

Apollodoros contends that Phrastor would never have recognized Phano's baby as legitimate if he had not been sick. The first proof he gives of this is that Phrastor married an Athenian woman very soon after his recovery:

> I will show you by a strong and very obvious proof that Phrastor would never have recognized the child if he had been healthy. For as soon as he recovered from that illness and he felt better and was reasonably strong, Phrastor married a citizen woman in accordance with the laws, the legitimate daughter of Satyros of the deme Melite, the sister of Diphilos. Let *this* be evidence for you that he would not voluntarily have accepted Phano's child if he had not been compelled by his illness

and childlessness and by the women's nursing of him and his animosity toward his relatives, so that they not inherit his property. (§58)

The logic behind Apollodoros' proof is transparently weak. He suggests, without spelling it out, that Phrastor married again specifically for the purpose of producing legitimate heirs—which may or may not be true—and that he needed to do this because he recognized that Phano's child was not legitimate. These assumptions are not defended, however, and Apollodoros' explanation for Phrastor's marriage is neither obvious nor inevitable. The fact that Phrastor married again soon after his recovery can tell us nothing about whether he believed his son by Phano was a legitimate Athenian citizen.

Apollodoros' second proof has to do with the difficulties Phrastor experienced when he attempted to enroll his son by Phano into his phratry and genos. (Like the phratry, the genos was a kinship group to which only legitimate male citizens could belong.) When Phrastor introduced the child to these associations, his fellow *gennetai* (the members of his genos) refused to admit the boy. Apollodoros conjectures that they denied him entry because they knew that the child's mother was Phano, Neaira's daughter, and they knew about the divorce, and they knew that Phrastor had recognized the boy as legitimate only when he was near death (§59).[15]

If Phrastor met with resistance when he introduced the child to his phratry and genos, however, it should not surprise us: he had, after all, initiated a proceeding against Stephanos alleging that the child's mother was an alien. Word of his suit and of its out-of-court settlement would surely have gotten around. The gennetai and phratry members who rejected Phano's son were probably responding to the rumors that had been created or exacerbated by Phrastor's aborted litigation. We need not believe that they had access to any more certain information about Phano's parentage.

Phrastor was not willing to let the matter drop when his son was rejected. He responded by bringing suit against his genos, and the issue ended up before a public arbitrator. Phrastor's actions at the arbitration hearing, Apollodoros tells us, prove that he had not recognized Phano's baby willingly but because he was forced by circumstances to do so: "The gennetai challenged Phrastor before the arbitrator to swear on sacrificial victims that he believed that his son had been born from a citizen woman to whom he had been married in accordance with the law. But when they proffered this challenge to Phrastor before the arbitrator, he did not take the oath, and he did not swear" (§60). Phrastor's refusal to swear is ostensibly damning. But several considerations suggest that Apollodoros is not telling us the whole truth here.[16]

First, it is likely that when introducing his son to his phratry Phrastor was required to swear an oath similar to the one mentioned here, stating that the child was born from a duly married citizen wife. If so, Phrastor should have been prepared to swear as much before the arbitrator as well, and his alleged reluctance to do so is odd.[17]

Second, Apollodoros introduces members of Phrastor's genos to testify and substantiate his account. If the deposition of the gennetai that has been preserved in the speech is authentic, however, then all that these men testified to, in fact, was that the genos had originally rejected Phrastor's son. They do not tell the jurors about the results of the arbitration proceeding: "Timostratos of Hekale, Xanthippos of Eroiadai, Eualkes of Phaleron, Anytos of Lakiadai, Euphranor of Aigilia, and Nikippos of Kephale depose that they and Phrastor of Aigilia are members of the genos called the Brytidai; and when Phrastor asked to introduce his son into the genos, they prevented him from introducing the boy, knowing that he was the son of Phrastor by the daughter of Neaira" (§61).[18]

Finally, Apollodoros himself does not tell us what the result of the arbitration proceeding was. We know that Phrastor refused to take the oath, but are we to understand that his refusal brought the hearing crashing to a halt? Did it prompt the arbitrator to dismiss Phrastor's claim and decide in favor of the genos? That, clearly, is the implication of Apollodoros' account, but if it were true, would he not have told the jury explicitly that the gennetai had won the day on that occasion, and that a public arbitrator had as much as declared Phano and her son to be aliens?

It seems unlikely that Phrastor would have bothered to bring suit against his genos for failing to register his son if he were unwilling to swear that the boy was born from a citizen woman and qualified for citizenship. Why, then, did he refuse to take such an oath? I am persuaded by one scholar's suggestion that Apollodoros has not told us everything about the oath the gennetai tendered. We have seen in Chapter 3 that challenges over the torturing of slaves were not straightforward, and litigants were wise to refuse them rather than allow their cases to rest on a slave's ability to endure torment. A challenge to swear an oath, or to accept another's oath, could likewise be tricky. The gennetai, in Phrastor's case, presumably composed the oath to which they wanted him to swear and worded it in such a way as to benefit their case. In re-creating their oath Apollodoros may have left out a key clause. The prosecutor tells us, as we have seen, that Phrastor refused to swear "that he believed that his son had been born from a citizen woman to whom he had been married in accordance with the law" (§60). Phrastor may have been challenged instead to swear that the child was born to him by a citizen wife *other than Phano* to whom he had been legally married. Because he has misrepresented the oath, meanwhile, Apollodoros does not dare to elicit testimony from the gennetai about the arbitration proceeding, and they substantiate only his account of the initial refusal by the genos to register Phrastor's son. Apollodoros' failure to state explicitly that the arbitrator decided in favor of the gennetai and that Phrastor's son was never admitted into his father's phratry and genos suggests in turn that the child *was* eventually accepted, and that he was living as a citizen at the time of Neaira's trial. (The child was probably not old enough when Neaira was tried, however, to have been introduced already to his father's deme.)[19]

What Apollodoros tells us about Phano's marriage to Phrastor and its consequences fails to prove his contention that Phano was an alien and that her son was undeserving of citizenship. He therefore does not provide us—who have more leisure to consider the prosecutor's speech than the court that decided his case some two millennia ago—with compelling evidence that Phano was Neaira's daughter and that Stephanos broke the law when he gave her in marriage to Phrastor.

VI

HOUSEGUESTS

AND

HUSBANDS

Phano was now a divorced woman living in her parental home. The son she had had by Phrastor was presumably being raised in his father's oikos—children in Athens belonged more fully to their father's family than to their mother's—cared for by servants and by the citizen woman Phrastor had married soon after he recovered from his illness (§§57–58). Phano herself, after her brief marriage, was still quite young and certainly still marriageable, though the 3,000 drachmas that had been used as a dowry in her first marriage were no longer available to her: Phrastor, it will be remembered, was allowed to keep Phano's dowry by the terms of his out-of-court settlement with Stephanos.[1]

ENTERTAINING GUESTS

Sometime after Phano's divorce, perhaps in the mid- to late 350s, another incident occurred which would involve the family in litigation, or in aborted litigation. Neaira and Stephanos were acquainted with a certain Epainetos, who came from the island of Andros in the Aegean. Apollodoros tells us that Epainetos had been a lover of Neaira's. This may be true, but it is also possible that Apollodoros has tacked on that detail in order to make his story more sordid. Whatever the origin of the relationship, Epainetos used to visit Stephanos and Neaira whenever he was in town. On the occasion in question, he stayed with the couple in the country, having been invited by Stephanos to join them there for some religious sacrifice.[2]

Epainetos' visit, however, proved less than idyllic. Stephanos walked in on him while he was having sex with Phano. Whether Phano was Stephanos' daughter or Neaira's, she was living in his household and was under his legal protection. Stephanos acted as any kyrios who found himself in this position was allowed to act. He did not kill Phano's lover, as he might have, and as the enraged husband of Lysias' speech *On the Murder of Eratosthenes* in fact did (see Chapter 4). Nor did he inflict humiliating punishments on Epainetos. Rather, Stephanos held his guest captive and demanded that he pay a ransom of 3,000 drachmas to secure his release. Epainetos agreed to do so, and he offered two Athenian friends as sureties for his payment— men who would assume responsibility for the debt in the event that Epainetos failed to pay up. Stephanos released Epainetos on the understanding that he would pay the sum demanded (§§64–65).

These are the bare facts of the story to this point, divorced from the unsupported charges Apollodoros makes against Stephanos in his discussion of the incident. The story makes sense as it stands. Stephanos' response to finding Epainetos with a woman of his oikos was in keeping with Athenian practice. He was not particularly interested in humiliating Epainetos, or killing him, but he was not averse to demanding that Epainetos pay out of his pocket for his mistake. Stephanos—if Apollodoros is telling the truth about the amount of money demanded—required that Epainetos pay 3,000 drachmas, precisely the sum he had lost to Phrastor. Since the matter would not be aired in a public forum—coming to a financial agreement with Epainetos kept the incident out of the courts—he could hope to marry Phano off to another husband who was unaware of what had happened, using Epainetos' 3,000 drachmas as a dowry.

The spin Apollodoros puts on this skeletal story, however, changes dramatically one's impression of the incident. Apollodoros, first of all, prefaces his account by claiming that what happened was an example of Stephanos' "sordid greed" and wickedness in action. According to the prosecution, the entire episode was part of a plan Stephanos had hatched to extort money from Epainetos, and Phano was in on the con. Stephanos, we are told, invited Epainetos to the country *on the pretext* of performing a sacrifice, and there he surprised Epainetos in flagrante delicto with Phano. The implication is that their coupling was not a spontaneous episode onto which Stephanos stumbled, but rather an essential ingredient in the family's plot to swindle their unsuspecting house guest:

> Stephanos here plotted against Epainetos of Andros, an old lover of Neaira's who had spent a lot of money on her and who, because of his affection for her, used to stay with them whenever he came to Athens. Stephanos summoned Epainetos to the country on the pre-

text of making a sacrifice, and he caught Epainetos as a moichos [that is, committing moicheia, having sex with Phano] with the daughter of Neaira here. Stephanos intimidated him and extorted thirty minai from him. He accepted as sureties for this amount Aristomachos . . . and Nausiphilos . . . , and he let Epainetos go on the understanding that he would pay Stephanos the money. (§65)

We are in no position to say whether Apollodoros is right in claiming that Epainetos was the victim of a plot. Certainly Apollodoros' information is suspect, because he is attempting in his speech to portray Stephanos as a villain. The incident makes sense, moreover, without our assuming that Stephanos lured Epainetos to the country for the express purpose of catching him in bed with Phano. But certainty about what happened remains impossible.

ILLEGAL IMPRISONMENT

When Epainetos was released by Stephanos he did not pay his captor the promised 3,000 drachmas. Instead, he charged Stephanos with having illegally imprisoned him. Epainetos claimed that his detention by Stephanos had not been legal because he was not a moichos. While he admitted to having had sex with Phano, his intercourse with her did not constitute moicheia— a sexual offense against Phano's kyrios—because, he claimed, Phano was a prostitute and Stephanos' home was a brothel:

Epainetos admitted to having sex with the woman, but not that he was a moichos. For she was not the daughter of Stephanos, he said, but of Neaira, and her mother knew that Phano was involved with him. He had spent a lot of money on them, and whenever he was in town he supported the whole household. And he brought

97

forward against them the law which does not allow one to take a man as a moichos if he is with those women who sit in a brothel, or who sell themselves openly. He said that that was what it was, Stephanos' house, it was a brothel, and that was how they made most of their money. (§67)

We need not doubt that Apollodoros had access to a reasonably accurate account of the arguments Epainetos intended to make in court. The two men who stood surety for Epainetos and who, as we will see, later served as private arbitrators in the case, Aristomachos and Nausiphilos, were called by Apollodoros to give evidence at Neaira's trial (§71). They more than anyone were in a position to know the arguments Epainetos made either when he went before the magistrates to bring his indictment or later, when the matter was settled by arbitration. Epainetos, we may believe, did in fact claim that Phano was a prostitute and that her affair with him was known (at the least) to Neaira.

But were Epainetos' allegations true? Apollodoros does not offer any proof that Phano made a habit of entertaining men. Indeed, while he tells the jury what Epainetos' claims were, Apollodoros does not himself say that Phano was a prostitute, or that she had been sexually involved with anyone other than Phrastor and Epainetos. Probably, then, there was no dirt of this sort to dig up. As for Neaira's role in the seduction, we have no way of knowing whether she, let alone Stephanos, was aware that Phano was having sex with Epainetos.

Epainetos is unlikely to have been able to offer any solid evidence that Phano was a prostitute. But even if he could not bring before the court a string of satisfied clients to attest to Phano's debauchery, Epainetos may yet have had a chance of convincing a jury that his liaison with Phano fell short of moicheia. Phano, after all, had grown up with the notorious courtesan Neaira serving as her role model. A jury might well believe that Phano herself had taken to prostitution, or that the entire family was not above concocting just the sort of plot with which Apollodoros credits Stephanos.

Epainetos, then, might have won his case in court. If he did, he would be off the hook, owing nothing to Stephanos and free of any penalty for having had sex with Phano. Losing, however, was not a pleasant prospect to contemplate. The law under which Epainetos brought suit against Stephanos for illegal imprisonment detailed the punishment that an unsuccessful prosecutor in such a case—the alleged moichos—would receive: "If it is determined that the prosecutor is a moichos, his sureties are to hand him over to the man who caught him, and that man is to do to the prosecutor, as he would to a moichos, whatever he wishes in the courtroom, though not using a knife" (§66). A small consolation it must have been, when one's tormentor was wielding a radish, that the law forbid the use of knives.

Epainetos either was very sure that he would prevail in court or, more likely, he was betting that Stephanos would back down rather than allow the matter to become public. Indeed, Epainetos seems to have been playing the same game of chicken with Stephanos that Phrastor had played. The latter, when faced with a suit that would in all likelihood result in his owing Stephanos 3,000 drachmas, had brought a countersuit that threatened Stephanos' oikos: it called into question the citizenship status of Phano and her unborn child and jeopardized Stephanos' citizen rights and property. Epainetos likewise owed 3,000 drachmas to Stephanos, and he too sought to avoid payment by instituting a lawsuit.

It does not seem that Stephanos had much to lose from Epainetos' suit per se. From what Apollodoros tells us of the law on illegal imprisonment, Stephanos, if he lost the case, would not be punished for having detained Epainetos (though he would perhaps be vulnerable to subsequent prosecution by his former captive). Stephanos would, naturally, be out the 3,000 drachmas Epainetos had agreed to pay him, and he would not have the satisfaction of torturing Epainetos in the courtroom, but there would be no additional penalty. Stephanos *was* threatened by Epainetos' suit, however. Whether he won the case or not, the fact of Phano's promiscuity would be aired in a public forum. This would be more than a humiliating admission for Stephanos' family. It would, more important, damage Phano's prospects for a second marriage, if not destroy them entirely. Women who were (known to have been) found with moichoi in Athens lived afterward in disgrace, prohibited by law, for example, from attending public sacrifices, where they might associate with and corrupt respectable women. (See below.) Public disclosure of Phano's affair would be ruinous for her, and it might, besides, have damaged Stephanos' political career.[3]

Epainetos was taking a big chance to avoid losing 3,000 drachmas, but he may have known Stephanos well enough to guess that he would back down if threatened with the exposure of Phano's sexual misdeed: Stephanos, after all, had backed down before when he was threatened by Phrastor. In the end, Epainetos' gamble paid off. Stephanos agreed to submit the matter to private arbitrators, the same men, as it happened, who had been standing surety for Epainetos.

The arbitrators heard the case and arrived at what seems to have been an equitable decision:

> Stephanos was not able to make any legal argument, but he thought that Epainetos should make a contribution toward the marriage portion of Neaira's daughter. He spoke of his own lack of resources and of Phano's previous misfortune in her marriage with Phrastor. And he said that he had lost her dowry and he would not be able to marry her off again. "You have had relations with her," he said. "It would be right for you to do good by her in some way." He made other seductive argu-

ments too, things which someone who was begging and wanted out of a difficult situation might say. The arbitrators listened to both parties to the dispute and reconciled them, and they persuaded Epainetos to give 1,000 drachmas toward the marriage portion of Neaira's daughter. (§§69–70)[4]

Stephanos walked away from the bargaining table with a third of the money he had hoped to extract from Epainetos, and Epainetos paid a lower price than he might have for the pleasures he had extracted from Phano. More important, both parties had avoided the humiliation that a day in court would—or in Epainetos' case, could—bring. Their time before the arbitrators, it would seem, had been satisfactory for everyone concerned.

Apollodoros explains in his introduction to the Epainetos story that the affair provides further proof that Neaira was not an Athenian citizen: "Consider," he said, "the sordid greed and wickedness of Stephanos here, so you may know from it that this Neaira is not a citizen" (§64). The Epainetos story is the second of three proofs Apollodoros offers as evidence that Stephanos and others treated Phano as an alien rather than as a citizen. Phano's status, in turn, was intended as proof that Neaira was likewise an alien. As we have seen, however, Epainetos' allegations that Phano was Neaira's daughter and herself a prostitute were not necessarily true. These charges, moreover, are *not* corroborated by Stephanos' decision to settle out of court: it is hardly surprising that Stephanos was reluctant to air Phano's indiscretions in a public courtroom.

However ineffective a support for the prosecution's case, however, Apollodoros' account of the Epainetos story happily provides us with further tantalizing information about the problems Neaira and her extended family faced nearly twenty-five hundred years ago. We turn next to the troubles that attended Phano's second marriage.

DEMOCRATIC ROYALTY

Phano's marriage to Theogenes of the deme Erchia was a by-product of Stephanos' political machinations. Theogenes, according to Apollodoros, was a blue-blooded Athenian, fortunate as far as lineage went, but poor and inexperienced in political affairs. It happened that Theogenes was selected to serve in Athens for a year as archon basileus, or king archon (§72). This does not mean that he was to enjoy anything like regal authority. The office of the king archon was, according to tradition, a vestige of the ancient Athenian kingship (cf. §§74–75), but in the democracy of classical Athens the king's power, like that of any polis official, was limited and clearly defined. The duties of the archon basileus were primarily religious and judicial. It would be Theogenes' job during his year in office, for example, to superintend the Eleusinian Mysteries and to preside over courts trying cases of impiety.[5]

As with most Athenian magistracies, the office of the king archon was filled by sortition, double sortition, in fact, in the case of this and nine other magistracies (the "nine archons" and their secretary). Each of the ten Athenian tribes—geographically based subdivisions of the citizen body—selected by lot ten candidates for the ten offices to be filled, resulting in a total, polis-wide, of one hundred candidates. In a second lottery one candidate was selected from each tribal group, producing a final group of ten. One of these ten—Theogenes, in this particular year—would serve as *basileus*.[6]

Every candidate for office in Athens, whether selected by sortition or elected, underwent a preliminary scrutiny, or *dokimasia*, an examination of his formal qualifications for office. The candidate was asked a series of questions about his parentage, for example, and his military service, after which any citizen could lodge a complaint against him. Whether an accuser came forward or not, a vote was held and the candidate was either rejected or confirmed in office. The candidates for other magistracies in Athens underwent a preliminary scrutiny only once, but the archon basileus and the other eight of the nine archons were scrutinized twice, before two different bodies.[7]

Theogenes, as we said, was allegedly naive when it came to politics. But when the time came for him to undergo his scrutiny he had the help of a friend more seasoned in public affairs than himself. Stephanos, Apollodoros says, stood by Theogenes at his dokimasia. The result was that Theogenes was confirmed in his magistracy. When he entered into office Stephanos was ready to assist him again, helping Theogenes meet the expenses that came with his new responsibilities. As Apollodoros tells it, Stephanos' timely assistance was part of his attempt to ingratiate himself with the new basileus. Whether he in fact had ulterior motives in helping Theogenes or not, Stephanos did manage to secure Theogenes' good will. It was natural enough, after the help he had received, for Theogenes to appoint Stephanos as one of his two *paredroi*, associates who would assist the archon with his responsibilities during his year in office (§72).

The relationship between the archon basileus and his assistant would become closer still. Stephanos gave Phano in marriage to Theogenes sometime after the archon had entered into office and appointed Stephanos as his *paredros*. The divorcée and one-time lover of Epainetos thus settled into a new life as the wife of Athens' principal religious functionary.[8]

MARRIED TO THE KING

The wife of the archon basileus, called the *basilinna* or queen, herself played a prominent role in at least one of the state's religious festivals. During the three-day festival of the Anthesteria, which took place roughly in late February (the eleventh, twelfth, and thirteenth days of the Athenian month Anthesterion), the basilinna made secret offerings on the city's behalf and

administered an oath to the "venerable priestesses," who as-
sisted her in the sacred rites and would participate in other festivals. In what must have been the highlight of the Anthesteria,
the queen was "married" to the god Dionysos. There was a marriage procession from the sanctuary of Dionysos at the Marshes
(the site has not been identified) to the Boukoleion, the ancient
residence of the archon basileus. There the marriage of the basilinna to Dionysos was somehow "consummated," though the
details of that act are not known. The queen's union with the
god may have been achieved through actual intercourse with a
man (presumably her husband) impersonating Dionysos, or she
may have performed some kind of ritual with a herm that sym-
bolized the marriage's consummation. (The herm was a common form of statuary in Greece. With one obvious difference,
it looked like a large Pez dispenser: a stone pillar topped by a
bust, usually of the god Hermes, and sporting an erect phallus.
Herms, which were viewed as serving a protective function,
were placed throughout Athens at crossroads and in front of
houses.)⁹ (Fig. 11).

Apollodoros bristles at the thought that Phano, as the wife
of the archon basileus, had performed these sacred rituals. She
was, after all, an alien, or so he continues to claim, and she had
acted in the past in a way that made her an unacceptable representative of the city in its dealings with the god:

> This woman performed on behalf of the city the sacri-
> fices that are not to be named, and she saw things which
> it was not appropriate for her, as an alien, to see; and
> she, being the sort of woman she is, entered into places
> where no one of the great many Athenians except the

FIGURE 11. A herm, a peculiar type of Greek statuary found throughout Athens at crossroads and in front of houses.
Courtesy, Museum of Fine Arts, Boston. Gift of Landon T. Clay.

wife of the basileus enters; she administered an oath to the venerable priestesses, who assist with the sacrifices, and she was given as a wife to Dionysos; she performed on the city's behalf the many rites, holy and not to be named, that our ancestors handed down. If it is not possible for everyone to *hear* about these things, how is it duly reverent for just anyone to *perform* them, especially a woman of such a sort, who has done such things? (§73)

Stephanos and Neaira must have been proud of the little girl who had grown up and managed, despite her problematic episodes with Phrastor and Epainetos, to marry well and play such a prominent role in the city's religious life. As Apollodoros tells it, they should have been proud of themselves as well. This time around they had not only managed to trick Phano's citizen husband into marrying the daughter of a Corinthian whore, but they had pulled a fast one on the entire Athenian population, whose most sacred rites were now being celebrated by an alien debauchee. If Stephanos and Neaira *were* feeling self-congratulatory about their feat—and we will consider presently whether the incident provides evidence that Phano was indeed an alien—their mood cannot have lasted long.

Sometime after the celebration of the Anthesteria and before Theogenes left office—thus between late February and midsummer of the year in question (which cannot be precisely identified but was probably in the late 350s)—Theogenes' happy relationship with his new wife and father-in-law came crashing to a halt. The Areopagos Council (an august body in Athens which tried cases of premeditated homicide and wounding, arson, and fatal poisoning), presumably because the celebration of the Anthesteria had drawn attention to Theogenes' bride, looked into Phano's background and determined that she was not fit to perform the duties of the basilinna.

The Areopagites, according to Apollodoros, meant to keep the matter quiet, not wishing to make a scandal out of the recent celebration of the secret rites, perhaps, or wanting Theogenes to emerge from the incident with his reputation intact. (Apollodoros makes a point of mentioning the secrecy of the Areopagites' investigation, probably in order to explain to the jurors why they had never heard of this scandal previously.) But the council members did intend to impose a fine on the basileus, and they would have done so if Theogenes had not beaten them to the punch. Intent, it would seem, on making a show of his innocence, Theogenes offered to divorce Phano, and the council accepted his solution. When Athens' king archon returned home after his secret meeting with the Areopagites, he threw his wife out of the house and dismissed Stephanos from the *paredria* (§§80–83).[10]

NOT THE RIGHT KIND OF WIFE

What had happened? What did the Areopagites find out about Phano that made them ready to fine Theogenes and that prompted him to dissolve his relationship with Phano and Stephanos? There are several possibilities. Apollodoros tells us that there was an ancient law, evidently still in effect in the mid-fourth century, that set forth the qualifications for the wife of the basileus: "The Athenians introduced a law that the wife of the archon basileus was to be a citizen and was not to have had sex with another man, but he should marry a virgin, so that the sacrifices that are not to be named might be performed in accordance with tradition on the city's behalf, and so that the customary offerings might be made to the gods in accordance with piety, and so that nothing would be abolished and there would be no innovation" (§75). The wife of the archon basileus, then, had to be a citizen, and she had to have been a virgin when she married her husband. The Areopagites had evidently discovered in the course of their secret investigation of her that Phano did not meet one or both of these requirements. Either some evidence had come to light to suggest that she was Neaira's daughter, or the council had learned of her previous marriage to Phrastor or her affair with Epainetos.[11]

Apollodoros suggests that Phano was unsuitable as a basilinna both because she was an alien (§§73, 81) and because she had been taken in adultery with Epainetos (§§85–87). But in his dramatic retelling of Theogenes' audience with the Areopagites on that fateful day, Apollodoros portrays Theogenes as having spoken to them exclusively of his wife's citizenship status:

> They discussed the matter, and the Areopagos Council was displeased and ready to fine Theogenes because he had taken such a wife and allowed her to perform on the city's behalf the rites that are not to be named. But Theogenes begged, pleading and entreating, and said that he had not known that she was the daughter of Neaira. He said that he had been deceived by Stephanos and had married her in accordance with the law on the understanding that she was the legitimate daughter of Stephanos. He had made Stephanos, a man he considered well-disposed to him, his paredros because of his own inexperience in public affairs and his lack of guile, so that he could fulfill the duties of his office, and for the same reason he had become Stephanos' kinsman by marriage. "To show you that I am not lying," he said, "I will provide you with a great and clear proof. I will send the woman away from my house, since she is not the daughter of Stephanos but of Neaira. If I do this, let what I have said—that I was deceived—be accepted as trustworthy. If I don't, then punish me as a wicked man who is guilty of impiety against the gods." (§§81–82)

Apollodoros tells a good story, but he fails to provide convincing proof for his claim that the Areopagos found Phano unsuitable because of her citizenship status. He does not call any Areopagites to the stand to confirm his version of the events. (Admittedly, if the council was indeed intent on keeping the matter quiet, as Apollodoros claims, then the prosecutor may not have been able to persuade the Areopagites to testify on his behalf.) Apollodoros does introduce Theogenes' testimony to the court, which means that Theogenes testified to the truth of at least *some* of what Apollodoros had said, but we need not believe that he verified Apollodoros' account in all its particulars. A document that purports to be Theogenes' deposition but which may not be genuine has been preserved in the *Against Neaira*. If that document is genuine (or if it is an accurate reflection of the original document's content), then Theogenes did not in fact have anything to say about the reason for the Areopagites' discontent: "Theogenes of Erchia testifies that when he was basileus he married Phano on the understanding that she was the daughter of Stephanos, and when he learned that he had been deceived, he threw the woman out of his house and no longer lived with her, and he expelled Stephanos from the office of the paredros and did not allow him to continue to serve as his assistant" (§84). The deposition may seem at first glance to imply that what Theogenes had been deceived about was the claim that Phano was the daughter of Stephanos, but that impression is not borne out by a closer reading of the text. Precisely *how* Theogenes had been deceived is nowhere specified.[12]

Can we believe, then, that the Areopagites had indeed dredged up damning information about Phano's citizenship? Certainly we must discount Apollodoros' claims to that effect and confine ourselves to the positive statements he makes—that the Areopagites were ready to fine Theogenes because of the inquiry, but Theogenes responded by divorcing Phano and removing Stephanos from the paredria. Yet if we attempt to reconstruct the results of the Areopagites' inquiry from their and Theogenes' reactions to it, we turn up only a jumble of ostensibly contradictory conclusions. I confess that I have been unable to imagine a model of events that adequately explains the behavior of everyone involved.

On the one hand, the Areopagites' reaction to the information they uncovered suggests that they regarded Theogenes' offense as relatively minor. The council was ready to dispense with the matter, according to Apollodoros, by fining the basileus, admittedly with the largest fine permitted by law. But if they had thought it appropriate, the Areopagites could have referred the matter to a lawcourt for trial, where a guilty verdict might have brought a far more severe penalty.[13]

On the face of it, the Areopagites' reaction to the inquiry seems consistent with their having discovered that Phano had been married to Phrastor before she married Theogenes. Any investigation by the Areopagos was very likely to uncover information about Phano's first marriage. The marriage was, after all, something that people in the community would have known of and talked about. Phano's union with Phrastor, moreover, had produced a son whose introduction to his father's phratry and genos had caused a stir. Any number of people, observing Phano's public performance at the Anthesteria, could have questioned the seemliness of her participation in the rites and brought the matter to the Areopagites' attention. Her previous marriage would certainly have been considered an offense: according to the law Apollodoros cites in his speech, the basileus was supposed to marry a virgin. The Areopagites would have needed to punish Theogenes in some way upon discovering that Phano was a divorcée, and a fine may well have been deemed appropriate. We have no reason to think, at least, that Phano's offense would have warranted a harsher penalty.

If the Areopagites had uncovered information about Phano's relationship with Epainetos, however, it is unlikely that they would have been content with fining Theogenes. Women who had been caught with a moichos, as Apollodoros is happy to remind the jurors trying Neaira (§§85–86), were not allowed even to attend public sacrifices, let alone to perform them. If such a woman *did* attend a sacrifice the law prescribed, as Apollodoros puts it, that she "suffer whatever she suffers, with impunity, except for death" (§87). The orator Aeschines, referring to the same law, is more explicit: "The lawgiver does not allow the woman with whom a moichos is caught to adorn herself or to attend public sacrifices, so that she not corrupt the most faultless of women by associating with them. But if she does attend the sacrifices or adorn herself, then the lawgiver prescribes that any man who comes along is to tear off her clothes and rip off her adornments and beat her, except he cannot kill or maim her. The lawgiver, in so ordaining, brings disgrace on such a woman and makes her life intolerable." Clearly the Athenians were serious about excluding these tainted women from the city's religious events. Probably, if the Areopagites had known about the affair with Epainetos, they would have regarded Phano's performance of the sacrifices at the Anthesteria as a very serious offense indeed, and they would have responded accordingly.[14]

We would likewise expect the Areopagites to have responded differently if they had discovered that Phano was not in fact an Athenian citizen. Now, we cannot really know which of the two the Athenians would have found the more reprehensible, that a previously married woman had acted as basilinna or that an alien woman had. Insofar as both were transgressions of the law Apollodoros cites in his speech, they may have been perceived as comparable offenses against the gods. The difference between the two, however, is that, apart from the offense of Phano's performance as basilinna, Theogenes' marriage to an alien woman would have been inherently illegal. We would therefore expect that, however the Areopagites chose to punish Theogenes for the offense of having allowed an alien to perform at the Anthesteria, they would in addition have been ready to refer the matter to the lawcourt for further action.

The Areopagites' reaction to the inquiry, then, is consistent with their having learned of Phano's previous marriage only. But Theogenes' reaction suggests that what he was told about Phano both angered him and caught him off guard. Not content with submitting to a fine—or unwilling to submit to a fine—he rushed home from his meeting with the council, divorced his wife, and severed his relationship with Stephanos. Apollodoros tells us that Theogenes felt he had been deceived by Stephanos, and he certainly acted as if he had been. But deceived about what? It does not seem credible that Theogenes was unaware of Phano's previous marriage to Phrastor. Stephanos and Phano could scarcely have expected to hide that fact from Phano's second husband, particularly given the existence of a son, nor would there have been any obvious benefit for them in doing so. (Unless Stephanos had hoped to deceive the basileus only temporarily, so that Phano would have a chance to perform as basilinna. But to what end?) Theogenes, confronted by the Areopagos with the fact of Phano's first marriage, may have been annoyed to find himself rebuked by the council on account of his wife, but would he have divorced her for that reason? Theogenes' behavior suggests rather that the Areopagos had found out about Epainetos or discovered that Phano was not an Athenian citizen. His reaction to the inquiry, in other words, does not mesh with that of the Areopagites.

Other questions arise in connection with Phano's celebration of the Anthesteria. Why, for example, was she allowed to perform the rites at all, since her previous marriage to Phrastor, if nothing else, rendered her an unsuitable celebrant? Can Stephanos and Theogenes have been ignorant of the law concerning *basilinnai*? Can it be that no one involved in the festival had bothered to check on the qualifications of the basilinna prior to her performance of the rites? Or were Stephanos and Theogenes trying—for reasons we can only guess at—to pass Phano off as Theogenes' virgin bride? In the end we simply cannot know the full story of Phano's participation in the rites, maddening though that is.

We cannot be sure, either, whether Phano was Neaira's daughter. If we believe that she was, then we must also believe that Stephanos was foolish enough, or brazen enough, to give an alien woman in marriage to Athens' archon basileus. As basilinna, Phano would be one of the city's most public female figures, and the secret of her alien status would be for that reason more vulnerable to discovery. That Stephanos would willingly subject Phano to increased scrutiny strains credibility if she *was* an alien, but human beings, ancient and modern, do not always act rationally.

We can at the least conclude that Apollodoros has failed to prove his contention that Phano was Neaira's daughter and therefore not a citizen. But the fact that we cannot dismiss that possibility out of hand is a testament to the prosecutor's success at mudslinging. Twenty-five hundred years after the fact, some of the mud still sticks.

III

THE
TRIAL
AND
ITS
ANTECEDENTS

VII

THE

FEUD

Stephanos had a knack for be-
coming involved in legal disputes. We have seen already that
the years he spent with Neaira were riddled with lawsuits,
though many of them never came to trial. Early on in their relationship, Stephanos had defended Neaira against Phrynion's attempt to hale her into slavery. He was sued by Phrynion, and the
matter was settled eventually through private arbitration (§§40,
45–48). A short time later, in 369, Stephanos prosecuted the
poet Xenokleides for failing to serve on a campaign against the
Spartans. The case was probably politically motivated, but Apol-

lodoros adds the provocative detail that Xenokleides had been a lover of Neaira's when she lived in Corinth (§§26–27). Phano's marriage in the 350s to the sober-minded Phrastor ended in divorce and further legal repercussions—a suit for maintenance against Phrastor, Phrastor's countersuit against Stephanos, and an out-of-court settlement (§§51–54). Stephanos was sued by Epainetos for illegal imprisonment after he held his houseguest prisoner as a moichos and demanded ransom from him. That dispute too ended in private arbitration (§§64–71). And Stephanos was not directly involved in this brush with the law, but he watched from the sidelines while Phano was investigated by the Areopagos Council and found unsuitable to serve as Athens' basilinna (§§80–84).

There was also, of course, the trial against Neaira in the late 340s, the case for which Apollodoros wrote his speech and the reason we know anything at all about this notorious courtesan's life in retirement. But Apollodoros' prosecution of Neaira is one chapter only in a dispute between the protagonists that had been playing itself out on Athens' legal stage. Apollodoros and Stephanos, as we said earlier, had faced one another in court before.

THE OPENING SALVO

Athens was a notoriously litigious society, where feuds very often made their way to the courts, the principals in the dispute and their relatives and friends trading lawsuits with one another over a number of years. Apollodoros' quarrel with Stephanos is an example of this kind of drawn-out affair, and Stephanos— the prosecution makes clear to the court—had fired the first shot.[1]

The first chapter of their dispute was tied up with some of the most important political questions of the day—how the Athenians should respond to the aggression of Philip II of

Macedon, Alexander the Great's father, and how, given a chronic shortage of money, the city would finance its military expeditions. In the 350s Philip had begun his steady march toward dominance in the Greek world, first securing his position within Macedon itself, then expanding his power through conquests in northern Greece. He took Amphipolis and Pydna in 357, for example, Krenides (which he renamed Philippi) in 356, and Pydna's northern neighbor Methone (where Philip lost an eye when he was struck by an arrow) in 354. In the autumn of 348, too, despite the military support—too little and too late—that the Athenians had offered Macedon's latest victims, Philip took Olynthus, on the Chalcidic peninsula. The city was razed and its population was enslaved.[2]

But in the summer of 348, when Apollodoros' feud with Stephanos was about to erupt, saving Olynthus had still been possible. The Athenians at that time were on the verge of sending an army north in support of the city. They were also about to dispatch reinforcements to Euboea, where the Athenians had been trying to prop up the regime of one of that island's tyrants. With this as the political backdrop, Apollodoros, who had been selected by lot to serve for the year as one of Athens' five hundred council members, proposed a decree that was subsequently put to the vote in the Athenian assembly. He proposed that the assembly decide whether the city's surplus monies should be allocated to Athens' military fund or to the Theoric fund (§§3–4).

The Theoric fund is a poorly understood institution. It had begun life as a subsidy for poor Athenians who could not afford to attend the city's dramatic festivals. (This origin is reflected in the fund's name: the *theorika*, the theoric monies, were distributed to pay for the attendance of the poor at *theoriai*, public spectacles in the theater.) In the mid-fourth century, however, the fund had grown in importance under the leadership of the statesman Euboulos. Money allocated to the fund came to be used not only for the purchase of theater tickets but for other purposes as well, such as construction work. The Theoric fund became a kind of sacred cow. Indeed, at some point—it is not clear whether this law was already in force when Apollodoros made his proposal—it became illegal even to *propose* the transfer of monies from the Theoric fund to Athens' military fund. One source tells us that anyone making such a proposal would face the death penalty.[3]

The Theoric fund, because of its relation to the military fund, was also a bone of contention between those Athenians who advocated a more aggressive policy toward Philip of Macedon (and wanted money available for the purpose), such as the orator Demosthenes, and those who, like Euboulos, were less hawkish. Apollodoros' proposal, although he did not advocate outright an increase in the allocation to the military fund, suggests that he sided with Demosthenes in his support for an aggressive campaign against Philip.[4]

Apollodoros introduced his proposal to the Athenian assembly, and the assemblymen present voted to enact the decree. That is, the Athenians decided by vote that they would on some subsequent occasion vote on the disposition of Athens' surplus revenue. Some time later, perhaps at the next assembly meeting, the Athenians did just that. We are told that their decision to direct Athens' surplus into the city's military fund was unanimous (§5).[5]

STEPHANOS' INDICTMENT

Despite the apparent popularity of his decree, Apollodoros was vulnerable to prosecution as its proposer. As we mentioned already in Chapter 4, anyone who introduced a motion before the assembly was held accountable for it and could be punished (although the Athenians who rendered a decree authoritative with their votes assumed no legal responsibility). Any Athenian citizen who wanted to (and who had not lost his right to do so by, for example, becoming a debtor to the state) could indict a proposal on the grounds that it was illegal or otherwise injurious to the people. The prosecutor did so by bringing against the proposer a *graphe paranomon,* an "indictment for [proposing] illegal [measures]." The action could be brought at any time—before the vote on the motion, while it was being considered by the assembly, or anytime after it was passed. The indictment had the effect of suspending the proposal or decree pending a decision about its legality in an Athenian court. Decrees that were found by a jury to be inexpedient or in opposition to Athens' standing statutes were repealed. If the graphe paranomon was brought within a year of the decree's passage, its proposer too was liable to punishment, a situation which, as we said in Chapter 4, prompted many a politician to find third parties to introduce proposals on their behalf.[6]

Stephanos indicted Apollodoros' decree within a year of its passage, sometime after the Athenians voted to allocate surplus revenue to the military fund (§5). We are too ignorant about this incident and about the laws governing the Theoric fund to know on what arguments he based his attack. We are told in the prosecution's speech against Neaira that Stephanos accused Apollodoros of having proposed the decree at a time when he was in debt to the state and was for that reason forbidden by law to participate in politics. Stephanos may have alleged as much as part of his case against Apollodoros, but it is unlikely that the allegation was his principal complaint, and it is difficult to believe that the charge was true. Apollodoros was a wealthy man. Given that debtors to the state could not legally participate in political activities until their debts were paid, it would not make sense for him to have left unpaid a public debt he was capable of settling. Apollodoros was also regularly involved in politics, and he had been serving in the Athenian council at the time he made his proposal. Any long-standing public debt would likely have been found out already when he underwent his preliminary scrutiny for that position.[7]

Whatever his arguments, however, and although Apollodoros' proposal had been popular among the Athenians, Stephanos was persuasive. The jurors trying the case, at least 501 Athenians, determined in an initial vote that the decree should be rescinded and its proposer penalized. But because the action Stephanos had brought was an *agon timetos*, a lawsuit for which no penalty was defined by law, there was a second vote as well: the prosecutor and defendant each proposed a penalty, and the jurors decided between the two proposals.

There was no guarantee, naturally, that a prosecutor, having won his case, would prevail as well in the penalty round of an agon timetos. To do that he needed to propose a punishment that fit the jurors' attitudes toward the defendant more closely than his opponent's counterproposal did. A prosecutor in an agon timetos, in other words, needed to propose a penalty that was serious enough to satisfy his own lust for revenge, but not so harsh that a jury would reject it in favor of the defendant's less strict counterproposal. Convicted defendants, conversely, were wise to suggest a penalty that was not ridiculously lenient. (The philosopher Socrates, in his trial of 399, can only have angered jurors—if what Plato tells us about the trial is accurate in this particular—when he suggested that rather than suffering the penalty of execution proposed by the prosecutor, what he really deserved was to be maintained for the rest of his life at the state's expense.) In his trial against Apollodoros for proposing a decree that was contrary to the laws, Stephanos suggested as a penalty a fine of fifteen talents, or 90,000 drachmas. The jury preferred the defendant's counterproposal and fined Apollodoros one talent instead. As we will see later in this chapter, the prosecution in Neaira's trial made much of the enormity of the fine Stephanos suggested as a penalty in this case.[8]

Given the political background to Stephanos' graphe paranomon against Apollodoros—the Athenians' campaigns in Euboea and against Philip of Macedon and the disagreement
among Athenians about the disposition of surplus monies—it
has been supposed that Stephanos was acting on behalf of Euboulos or others who opposed Athens' involvement in large-
scale foreign expeditions. In other words, Stephanos may have
been playing the sycophant, bringing an indictment against
Apollodoros at the behest of some third party. If so, in doing
someone else's dirty work, Stephanos nonetheless won for himself a vendetta which would come in a few years to threaten
the security of his home with Neaira.[9]

MURDER IN APHIDNA

Stephanos was the aggressor also in the second round of his feud
with Apollodoros. Some time after his successful graphe paranomon, perhaps in 346, Stephanos charged Apollodoros with murder. He claimed that Apollodoros had gone in search of a runaway slave to the Attic deme Aphidna, about seventeen miles
from the city of Athens. There, in what circumstances we are
not told, Apollodoros allegedly struck and killed a woman.
Theomnestos, who was at the same time Apollodoros' son-in-
law and his brother-in-law, made some introductory remarks
to the jury at Neaira's trial prior to yielding the floor to Apollodoros: "Stephanos brought a false charge against Apollodoros,
saying that one time when he went to Aphidna searching after
a runaway slave of his, Apollodoros struck a woman and she
died from the blow. Stephanos got ready some slaves and disguised them as men from Kyrene [a city in north Africa], and
he proclaimed publicly a charge of murder against Apollodoros
at the Palladion [a temple of Athena southeast of Athens, just
outside the city wall]. And Stephanos here prosecuted the case.
He swore that Apollodoros killed the woman with his own

hand, and he imprecated destruction on Apollodoros and his race and his house" (§§9–10).[10]

The details Theomnestos provides suggest that Stephanos, in prosecuting Apollodoros, alleged that the dead woman had been a slave and that he had been her owner. First, there is the court in which the case was heard. Homicide in Athens was tried in one of five courts, depending on the nature of the case. (Whatever the locale of a murder trial, however, murderers were always tried outdoors. That way jurors and other participants in the trial did not have to be under the same roof as the defendant, who was thought to be polluted by bloodguilt.) The Areopagos Council, for example, that august body that had turned up its nose at Phano during her basilinna period, tried cases involving the intentional homicide of Athenian citizens. The court at the Palladion, however, where Apollodoros stood accused, heard cases of *bouleusis* (planning to cause death or planning an injury that resulted in death) and unintentional homicide as well as those involving the murder of slaves, resident aliens, and foreigners. What we are told of Apollodoros' alleged death blow suggests that bouleusis was not the issue considered by the court. And while the act Theomnestos describes may sound to us like voluntary manslaughter rather than murder (because Apollodoros did not necessarily intend to kill the woman), it would have been deemed intentional homicide under Athenian law: what seems to have mattered to the Athenians for the achievement of this classification was not the intent to kill but the intent to harm. The dead woman in Aphidna, it follows, was not an Athenian citizen killed unintentionally but was a foreigner, resident alien, or slave.[11]

Now, the prosecution of murder in Athens was not an affair in which the state usually involved itself. Legal action against a murderer (just as virtually all prosecutions) had to be undertaken by a private citizen rather than by a state-appointed prosecutor. Close relatives of the deceased were expected to prosecute on

behalf of their murdered family member, although citizens outside of this select group may have been allowed to prosecute as
well. If, however, the murderer's victim was a slave, the person
most likely to take legal action on the victim's behalf was the
slave's owner and not his relatives. As the prosecutor in the murder trial of Apollodoros, Stephanos probably was either a close
relative of the deceased or her master. Since it is unlikely that
Stephanos was related to a foreigner or metic, we may conclude
that he prosecuted in his capacity as the dead woman's owner.[12]

Perhaps more accurately, we may say that Stephanos
claimed that he was prosecuting in his capacity as the *alleged* victim's owner. From what Theomnestos tells us—and the details
he provides make his account credible—it seems that Apollodoros had not in fact been involved in a killing. Indeed, it may
be that no one was murdered at all: "Stephanos swore [in court]
to things that never happened, that he never saw, and that he
never heard about from anyone else. But he was caught swear-
ing falsely and bringing a false charge, and it was clear that he
had been hired by Kephisophon and Apollophanes, taking
money to get Apollodoros exiled or disfranchised. He received a
few votes from 500 drachmas, and he went off, having forsworn
himself and gained a reputation as a scoundrel" (§10).[13]

Stephanos' second attack on Apollodoros had not succeeded, or at least he had not succeeded in convicting Apollodoros on a charge of murder. We cannot know whether Stephanos had in fact expected to win the case. It may be that he,
or those on whose behalf he brought the charge, had wanted
merely to harass Apollodoros. Perhaps, too, Apollodoros' ene-
mies were interested in temporarily declawing him by keeping
him out of the courts and the agora, areas which murder sus-
pects were forbidden to enter.

As with Stephanos' earlier graphe paranomon, this case too
was probably politically motivated, though precisely what
scheming lay behind the attack cannot be uncovered. It is rea-

sonable to believe, though, that the trial was somehow connected with the Peace of Philokrates, signed between Athens
and Philip of Macedon in 346, and with the Athenian embassy
sent to Philip in that year. The Kephisophon who allegedly paid
Stephanos to bring the murder charge against Apollodoros may
have been the same Kephisophon, the son of Kallibios, who had
spoken in support of the Peace before the Athenian assembly
in 347. A certain Apollophanes, too, perhaps the same person
Theomnestos mentions, gave evidence in court in 343 about the
embassy to Philip. And Stephanos himself may have served in
346 as one of Athens' ambassadors. Some man named Stephanos, at least, went north to meet with Philip on that occasion. The three men who were behind the murder charge
against Apollodoros, in other words, can plausibly (if tenta-
tively) be associated with the political scene of 346. Their political machinations may well lie behind the trumped-up murder
charges Apollodoros faced at about the same time.[14]

Stephanos, whatever the political alliances motivating him,
had now attacked Apollodoros in court on two occasions. He
managed to get his adversary fined a talent in the first instance,
and he put Apollodoros through a lot of needless bother the
second time around. Apollodoros' dander was surely up, and
the situation was ripe for his revenge.

VENGEANCE IN THE COURTROOM

Revenging themselves against Stephanos, according to Theomnestos, was precisely what he and Apollodoros were after in
bringing suit against Neaira. Theomnestos is explicit on the
point. Indeed, that the trial was motivated by a desire for revenge is the principal idea Theomnestos wants to impress upon
the jurors hearing the case. He brings up the topic at once, in
the second sentence of his introductory speech to the jury:
"Many things prompted me, men of Athens, to bring this indict-

ment against Neaira and to come before you. For we suffered grave injustices at the hands of Stephanos, and we were thrust into the most serious dangers by him—my father-in-law and I and my sister and my wife—so that I am acting in this trial not as an aggressor but as one seeking vengeance; for this man initiated the quarrel, having never suffered any wrong at our hands either in word or deed" (§1).

In these same few words, in addition to introducing the theme of vengeance, Theomnestos makes two related points: the first is that Stephanos was the instigator of the quarrel that had led to the trial against Neaira; the second, its corollary, is that Theomnestos himself and Apollodoros had *not* acted aggressively. In emphasizing these opposed behaviors Theomnestos paints himself and Apollodoros as the ideal Athenian litigants, moderate citizens who had appealed to the court system only under compulsion, in response to the aggression of their adversary. Stephanos, by contrast, was too eager to litigate, too quick to abuse the system to achieve his ends.[15]

Contrary to what we might expect, revenge was considered by the Athenians to be a perfectly legitimate motive for prosecution. An accuser who was manifestly bringing charges because of his enmity toward a defendant could not be accused of sycophancy, of initiating the suit for personal gain. Litigants therefore regularly emphasized the bad blood between themselves and their opponents that had culminated in their appearance in court. On the other hand, Theomnestos needed to assure the jury that he and Apollodoros had not instigated the feud with Stephanos but were retaliating against the defendant for the wrongs they had suffered. Although they were the aggressors in *this* case, that is, they were, on the long view, the victims of Stephanos' outrageous legal assaults, and they had been compelled by a catalogue of their opponent's misdeeds to seek redress in a courtroom.[16]

Neaira, it should be remarked, is noticeably absent from all

of these considerations. She was not the real target of Apollodoros' attack. No one, not even the prosecution, pretended otherwise. And yet Neaira had the most to lose from the trial: if
Stephanos did not prevail in the case, she would be enslaved,
returned to the ignominious life she had pried herself out of
decades before. Nor could Neaira, because of her sex, speak in
her own defense at the trial: a woman who found herself sued
or having to sue in Athens was represented in court by a male,
usually her kyrios. Neaira thus sat impotent as Apollodoros
railed against her in the courtroom, naming her lovers and recit-
ing her family's embarrassments, a mute witness to the legal
maneuvering that might dramatically alter her life.

After introducing in his first sentences the subject of Stephanos' past behavior toward Apollodoros, Theomnestos spends
the rest of his time before the court, as we have seen, detailing
the wrongs Stephanos committed. His discussion of the murder
charge Stephanos brought against Apollodoros is fairly straightforward. But in discussing the defendant's first hostile act, the
graphe paranomon of 348, Theomnestos finds himself having
to walk a tightrope. Apollodoros, it will be remembered, had
lost that case. A jury of Athenian citizens had been persuaded
by Stephanos that Apollodoros' decree was illegal, and they had
fined Apollodoros a talent as a result. Criticism of Stephanos'
graphe paranomon might well be taken as criticism of the jurors'
decision in that case. This might in turn have antagonized
Neaira's jury, even if none of the dicasts trying her case had
served as jurors also on the previous occasion. But Theomnestos
was quick to exonerate the jurors: "Even nowadays, if the subject comes up somewhere, everyone agrees that Apollodoros
gave the best advice [in proposing his decree] and suffered un-
justly [in losing the graphe paranomon and being penalized].
So it is right to be angry at the man who deceived the jurors
with his speech and not at those who were deceived" (§5).

Theomnestos could not go very far in criticizing the outcome of the trial, but it was possible for him to castigate Stephanos in connection with the case in a manner that in no way denigrated the jury: he made a big to-do about the size of the fine Stephanos had proposed as a penalty. (In §8 Theomnestos explicitly absolves the jury of any blame in connection with Stephanos' proposed fine: "I am very grateful to the jurors who were trying the case then, because they did not allow Apollodoros to be plundered, but they fined him a talent, so that he was just able to pay it.") If the jurors had elected to impose Stephanos' fifteen-talent fine, Theomnestos explains, it would have meant ruin for Apollodoros and his extended family:

> When the jurors were taking a vote on the penalty, although we pleaded with him, Stephanos was not willing to yield. He proposed a fine of fifteen talents so that Apollodoros and his children would be disfranchised, and so that my sister [Apollodoros' wife] and all of us would fall into the greatest poverty and utter destitution. For Apollodoros' property was not quite worth three talents, so he would not have been able to pay such a large fine. And if the fine was not paid by the ninth prytany [a prytany was one tenth of the Athenian year], the debt would have been doubled and Apollodoros would have been recorded as owing thirty talents to the state. When he was inscribed as a debtor to the state, what property Apollodoros had would have been listed as public, and when it was sold, he and his children and his wife and all of us would have fallen into the most extreme poverty. Furthermore, Apollodoros' other daughter [that is, the one who was not already married to Theomnestos] would have been unmarriageable. Who would ever take as wife an undowered daughter from a man who was a debtor to the state and was impoverished? (§§6–8)

Theomnestos is exaggerating here in at least two respects. First, Apollodoros would indeed have been disfranchised as a result of his debt to the state, but his children would have inherited their father's debt and disfranchisement only if he died before paying what he owed. They would not themselves have been disfranchised prior to Apollodoros' death. Second, it is highly unlikely that Apollodoros' property amounted to only three talents. He had inherited a fortune of more than forty-three talents from his father Pasion, who died in 370 or 369. Even if Apollodoros had thrown away his money in fistfuls, it is unlikely that he could lay claim to only three talents two decades later. But it made a better story if Apollodoros had almost been ruined by Stephanos. Exaggerating the damage Stephanos might have inflicted on Apollodoros and his family, that is, was in keeping with Theomnestos' tactic of portraying Stephanos as the aggressor in the feud and Apollodoros as the victim.[17]

Trying Neaira for living with Stephanos as his wife provided the victimized Apollodoros with the opportunity to strike back at his adversary. But was the prosecution's desire for vengeance the only motive behind the attack? Stephanos' prosecutions of Apollodoros appear to have been politically motivated, even if we cannot identify precisely what the purposes behind them were. While we should not discount vengeance as a motivating factor in *this* case, Apollodoros' counterpunch may also have had a political dimension. Apollodoros dragged Stephanos and Neaira into court sometime between 343 and 340. He reviled the couple's lifestyle against a backdrop of growing Athenian hostility to Macedon. The orator Demosthenes, ever suspicious of Macedonian intentions, was at the peak of his influence during the period. There was growing disenchantment with the peace the Athenians had signed with Philip in 346. And appearing as witnesses for the prosecution in the course of Neaira's trial were none other than Euboulos (§48), who had probably instigated Stephanos' graphe paranomon against Apollodoros in

348, and Demosthenes himself (§123), who would have been in support of the decree Stephanos attacked. The relationships among the principals are tangled, their political aims impossible to make out. But probably more was going on in court on the day of Neaira's trial than the simple pursuit of vengeance. Neaira herself, the aging courtesan about whom the fuss only ostensibly was being made, sat and watched the show.[18]

VIII

SUPPORTING

CHARACTERS

We know something now about the former courtesan whom Apollodoros haled into court in the late 340s. She had grown up a slave in a Corinthian brothel, endured an abusive relationship in her twenties with a party-hopping Athenian, prostituted herself as a freelancer in Megara, and finally settled into three decades of a comparatively tranquil life with Stephanos, who would speak in her defense in court. But we have yet to look in any detail at the prosecutorial team of Theomnestos and Apollodoros.

THEOMNESTOS

Of the two men prosecuting Neaira it was in fact Theomnestos who had brought the charges against her, though it is clear that he did so at the instigation of Apollodoros. Theomnestos, the son of Deinias of the deme Athmonon, was, as we have said, Apollodoros' relative by marriage. One of Theomnestos' two sisters was married to Apollodoros, and Theomnestos had himself married the daughter born of that union, his own niece (§2). (Marriages between such close relatives were not uncommon in ancient Greece.) Theomnestos, fittingly enough, was younger than his father-in-law. He had been born probably around 380, while Apollodoros was born sometime between 395 and 393. At the time of Neaira's trial Theomnestos was in his late thirties.[1]

In initiating the suit against Neaira, Theomnestos had accepted formal responsibility for the prosecution. It was he rather than Apollodoros, for example, who would be fined 1,000 drachmas if the prosecution failed to win a fifth of the jurors' votes—a standard penalty hanging over the heads of prosecutors bringing certain types of lawsuits.

Athenian litigants were required, de facto if not de jure, to speak in court themselves. (Women, of course, were represented in court by their *kyrioi*.) They could not hire professional advocates to plead their cases for them, and indeed to receive money for speaking in court was a prosecutable offense. Athens may have been a litigious society, but it was no place for lawyers. Litigants could, however, receive help from unpaid fellow speakers, or *synegoroi*, friends or relatives of the litigant, at least in theory, who would speak in court during a part of the time that was allotted to the disputant. Athenians who lacked confidence or an aptitude for public speaking could thus escape to an extent the terrors of a live, solo performance before an audience of hundreds, and litigants very frequently appealed to synegoroi for assistance.[2]

In his capacity as the prosecutor of record, therefore, Theomnestos was required to address the court, at least briefly. He delivered the first fifteen of the 126 paragraphs of the speech Apollodoros wrote for the trial, or perhaps 10 percent of the speech's total of 8,195 words. As we have seen, he provided the court with background information about Apollodoros' feud with Stephanos—the graphe paranomon of 348, the fine of fifteen talents Stephanos proposed in that trial, and the charge that Apollodoros had killed a woman in Aphidna. Theomnestos also sought to answer the question the jurors could be assumed to be thinking—so why are *you* prosecuting instead of Apollodoros? Theomnestos claimed, exaggerating, that in seeking to destroy Apollodoros, Stephanos had nearly brought the entire family to ruin. Theomnestos was thus himself a victim, entitled to an interest in avenging himself on Stephanos. He suggests that the means he adopted for obtaining that vengeance—the attack on Neaira—had a kind of poetic justice to it: "Just as Stephanos here tried to deprive me of my relatives, contrary to your laws and decrees, so I too have come before you to show that this man is living in marriage with an alien woman, contrary to the law" (§13). If Stephanos was out to ruin Theomnestos' relatives, then Theomnestos would strike back at his adversary indirectly by attacking *his* family.[3]

Despite Theomnestos' explanations, it is not in fact clear why he rather than Apollodoros was bringing the case. Given Apollodoros' conspicuous participation in the trial, Theomnestos' role as prosecutor does not seem to have been intended to conceal the fact of his father-in-law's interest in the case. Nor does it seem that Apollodoros had wanted to delegate the responsibility of preparing the case to a henchman. Theomnestos' role in the proceedings was minimal, while Apollodoros both wrote the prosecution speech and delivered the bulk of it himself. It may be that Apollodoros did not have the right to bring this particular kind of suit, a *graphe xenias* (a suit against an alien for pretending to be a citizen): some scholars argue that a prosecutor who failed to get a fifth of the votes in a *graphe* (roughly translated, a public suit), in addition to being penalized with a 1,000-drachma fine, lost the right to bring that type of graphe in the future. Alternatively, Apollodoros may have been acting to keep his prosecutorial options open for the future. Theomnestos, probably less politically active than his father-in-law, had less need of preserving his right to bring particular types of lawsuits.[4]

Whatever the advantages to his bringing the case, Theomnestos did what he had to do to keep peace in the family. He attempted in his brief remarks to the jurors to solicit their sympathy for Apollodoros and to portray Stephanos as the real aggressor in the case. He closed his speech a short while after he had begun by explaining to the jurors that he needed to yield the floor to a more experienced *synegoros:* "I ask you, gentlemen of the jury, what I think it is fitting for a man to ask who is young and without experience in public speaking, that you allow me to call Apollodoros as my synegoros in this case. He is older than I am, you see, and more familiar with the laws, and he has paid careful attention to all of this. He was wronged by Stephanos here too, so that there is nothing wrong with him revenging himself on the one who started it" (§§14–15). And then Apollodoros mounted the speaker's platform.

APOLLODOROS, SON OF PASION

Apollodoros, as we have seen, regaled the jury with a lurid account of Neaira's dalliances and Phano's marriages. When he was finished with this narrative section of his speech, Apollodoros devoted a large part of what remained of his time before the court to expounding on Stephanos' cavalier treatment of

Athens' citizenship laws (§§88–106). Apollodoros expressed outrage that Stephanos had flouted the laws by treating Neaira and Phano as citizens and by insinuating Neaira's sons into the citizen registers: "The Athenian citizen body, you see, has sovereign authority over everything in the polis, and it is possible for it to do whatever it wants. Yet the citizens considered the grant of Athenian citizenship to be so fair and solemn a gift that they imposed laws on themselves governing what they must do to grant someone citizenship if they want to—laws which have now been dragged through the mud by Stephanos here and those who have contracted marriages as he has" (§88).[5]

If the prosecution's charge that Stephanos had violated Athens' citizenship laws is true, we can understand why Apollodoros—Apollodoros of all people—would have felt some annoyance. As it happens, our staunch defender of enfranchisement standards was himself the son of a slave, but *his* family had won Athenian citizenship the old-fashioned way: they had earned it by spending enormous sums of money on the city's behalf.

Apollodoros' father Pasion had been the slave of two Athenian bankers, Archestratos and Antisthenes. Pasion was trusted by them and rose to a position of responsibility in the bank. He was eventually granted his freedom and came to be the owner of the bank himself, though it is not clear in what order the two events occurred. As a freedman, Pasion enjoyed metic status in Athens. In the early 390s he married a certain Archippe, probably also a metic herself, and in the middle years of that decade Apollodoros was born, the older of the couple's two sons. (Apollodoros' brother Pasikles was born around 380.)[6]

Pasion managed to amass a fortune from his banking business, and he funneled large chunks of it back into the community. Apollodoros says in a speech he delivered around 351, for example, that his father had once donated one thousand shields to the Athenians—Pasion owned a shield factory—and that he had on five separate occasions paid for the manning and operation of an Athenian warship. We do not know in what years Pasion bestowed these particular gifts, but it was munificence such as this that won for him the Athenians' goodwill. He was rewarded with a grant of citizenship sometime between 394 and 376. Pasion's sons were enfranchised by the same decree (§2).[7]

When Pasion died in 370 Apollodoros was twenty-four years old. Though a young man (a decade or more younger than Theomnestos would be at the time of Neaira's trial), he became involved in litigation almost at once. He was sued shortly after Pasion's death by a certain Kallippos in connection with his father's banking business. Kallippos, who acted as a sort of ambassador in Athens for the polis of Heraklea on the Black Sea, had been trying for a number of years to get his hands on money a Herakleote merchant had deposited in the bank shortly before he was captured and killed by pirates. The speech Apollodoros delivered in court for this trial, and which he probably also wrote, has been preserved in the Demosthenic corpus as 52 *Against Kallippos*. We do not know whether Apollodoros was successful in this first foray into the Athenian lawcourts. Certainly the experience did not dissuade him from further legal adventures. Indeed, once started on his life as a litigant, Apollodoros seems to have been unwilling to leave the courtroom. His history is studded with legal actions, with Apollodoros appearing as both prosecutor and defendant, the slave's son and naturalized citizen endeavoring to outdo the Athenians by outsuing them.[8]

Not long after Kallippos' suit came to court, for example, Apollodoros became involved in a complex set of legal actions connected with his neighbor and one-time friend Nikostratos. This Nikostratos, while out one day in pursuit of runaway slaves, had been captured by an Aeginetan ship and sold as a slave himself. (This is the sort of thing that could happen when one traveled abroad at a time when international law was nonexistent.)

He managed to borrow money from strangers in order to ransom himself, but the terms of the loan he contracted were usurious. If he did not repay the money within a month, his debt would be doubled. Apollodoros lent Nikostratos money on this occasion, but afterward the relationship between them soured. Nikostratos and his brothers allegedly turned against Apollodoros, hoping in that way, Apollodoros claimed, to get away with not paying him back. The feud led to some ugliness. The brothers sicced a young vandal on Apollodoros' rose-beds, for example, and Nikostratos himself attacked Apollodoros one night near Athens' stone quarries. It led as well to a number of lawsuits. Among these was the trial in about 366 for which Apollodoros wrote his speech *Against Nikostratos,* our source for the details of the quarrel.[9]

Other suits followed. On more than one occasion Apollodoros went to court to recover debts owed to his father's estate. Among these cases was Apollodoros' prosecution in about 362 of the famous general Timotheos, who had borrowed money from Pasion in the 370s. The speech Apollodoros wrote and delivered on that occasion has been preserved as [Demosthenes] 49 *Against Timotheos.*[10]

Apollodoros was also involved more than once in litigation against his mother's second husband, Phormion, who had at one time been a slave of Apollodoros' father. Phormion was freed by Pasion, and he spent some years as a freedman running the bank and shield factory. When Pasion died, Phormion got the girl: as was sometimes done, Pasion bequeathed Archippe to Phormion in his will. Phormion and Archippe were married in accordance with the will's provision in 368 or 367, while Apollodoros himself was off on campaign, serving as the captain (trierarch) of an Athenian warship. Apollodoros was so angry when he came home to find the marriage a fait accompli that he brought charges against Phormion, though he abandoned the case before it went to court. After Archippe died in 360, Apollodoros sued Phormion in connection with her estate. His long-running feud with his stepfather erupted in court also in the late 350s, when Apollodoros charged Phormion with having misappropriated money from the family bank during the previous decade. A number of speeches connected with this round of their dispute are extant: Demosthenes 36 *For Phormion*, a speech delivered by a third party in support of Phormion, and Demosthenes 45 and 46, *Against Stephanos I* and *II*. Both of these were delivered by Apollodoros, and the *Against Stephanos II* was probably written by him as well rather than by Demosthenes.[11]

Phormion seems to have brought out the worst in his stepson. Apollodoros was vicious in his attacks in court. In one of the speeches Apollodoros delivered in connection with the feud, he repeatedly berates Phormion for his servile origins, mocking him, for example, for his foreign accent. We can perhaps understand Apollodoros' bitterness. He clearly hated his stepfather and resented him for having married Archippe. But given Apollodoros' own status as the enfranchised son of a former slave, his harping on Phormion's status in the speech seems ill advised at best. In attacking his stepfather, Apollodoros managed also to alienate himself from his brother Pasikles. He went so far as to claim in court that Pasikles had been fathered by Phormion rather than Pasion. (Pasikles, it will be remembered, was born some ten years before Pasion's death, so Apollodoros' charge was particularly scandalous.) One wonders if the brothers' relationship ever recovered after that charge was made.[12]

Another series of lawsuits arose in connection with one of the many liturgies Apollodoros performed. The liturgy in Athens was a peculiar sort of tax levied on the wealthy, who, rather than surrendering to the state some percentage of their property or income, were required to meet certain state expenditures. The liturgy, however, was ordinarily more than a financial burden, as a liturgist was required also to perform administrative duties in connection with the expenditure for which he had become responsible. One of the more well-known liturgies in Athens was the *choregia*, which required the liturgist to undertake the expense of staging a comedy or tragedy, for example, at one of the city's festivals. The liturgist performing the choregia, the choregos, was responsible at the same time for training the chorus that would perform in the production. The liturgy we know Apollodoros to have performed repeatedly was the trierarchy. Trierarchs were required to pay many of the expenses of operating one of the state's warships. The amount a trierarch wound up paying in the performance of his liturgy could vary considerably, depending in part on how lavish the liturgist chose to be, but it amounted to a substantial outlay in the thousands of drachmas. Trierarchs, too, unless they paid someone else to do the job for them, were required to serve as captains of the ship they were financing.[13]

Because of his wealth Apollodoros was required to perform liturgies frequently, and when he did so he evidently spared no expense, taking the view, or so he claimed, that he owed the Athenians for their grant of citizenship. He served as trierarch on several occasions. We hear of trierarchies performed by him in 368, 365, 362, and 356, while in 352 Apollodoros was the choregos of a boys' choir that performed at the festival of Dionysos.[14]

Apollodoros' trierarchy of 362 led to a spate of lawsuits. He sued a certain Polykles for the reimbursement of expenses he had incurred when he served as trierarch some five months beyond his allotted time. Polykles, Apollodoros' appointed successor, had rudely refused during that period to join the ship and take up the trierarchy. The speech Apollodoros wrote for the trial is preserved as [Demosthenes] 50 *Against Polykles*. Apollodoros also brought to court a number of the generals and other officers who had been in command during that problematic trierarchy.[15]

More could be said about Apollodoros' history of litigation, but what we have seen is surely sufficient to indicate that Apollodoros spent much of his time either in court or preparing for lawsuits: disputes arising from his family's banking business sometimes required legal settlement; his political ambitions landed him in court on occasion, as in the case of Stephanos' graphe paranomon over the decree of 348; and, we may be inclined to conclude, he was an obnoxious fellow who could not keep from quarreling with his neighbors and family. His feud with Stephanos, at any rate, and the series of legal actions that it led to, was nothing out of the ordinary for Apollodoros. He was more than equal to the tasks of defending himself against Stephanos' legal harassment and repaying his adversary in the same coin.

THE JURORS

In addition to the defendants and the prosecution team of Theomnestos and Apollodoros there was also, of course, a third actor in the drama of Neaira's trial, the large panel of jurors before whom the litigants performed. What, then, was the experience of these jurors in the court, and what role did they play in the trial?

Given our familiarity with modern judicial practices, we cannot help but to approach questions like these having certain preconceptions. Citizens impaneled to hear a modern trial are expected to remain at all times staid and seated behind their partition, twelve passive jurors in two straight lines. The experience of Athenian jurors could not have been more different.

We said at the outset of this book that the jury hearing Neaira's case was composed of 501 jurors. This was the smallest possible panel for the type of case Theomnestos and Apollodoros brought, a graphe (public suit) as opposed to a *dike* (private suit). For important *graphai* the jury could be even larger, increasing in size in increments of five hundred, with one odd juror added to preclude the possibility of a tie vote. We hear of cases tried by juries of 1,001, 1,501, 2,001, and 2,501, and in one case a court was convened with 6,000 jurors. *Dikai,* on the other hand, were tried by panels of 201 or 401 jurors depending on the amount of money that was at issue in the case.[16]

It perhaps goes without saying that with jury panels this large there was no possibility of a voir dire-type procedure, with the litigants interviewing and rejecting from the panel jurors who were deemed biased, for example, or otherwise unsuitable to try the case. There was, indeed, no expectation that the jurors would be unfamiliar with the events at issue or unacquainted with the litigants themselves. The jurors did, however, undergo a complicated selection procedure that was designed to minimize the likelihood of effective jury tampering.

Six thousand Athenian males, fully enfranchised citizens over the age of thirty who had volunteered for the task, were sworn in annually to serve as jurors for the duration of the year. Each juror was issued a *pinakion,* a ticket that would be used in the selection of dicasts for particular cases. Depending on the year they were produced, these *pinakia* were made of bronze or boxwood (the Athenians shifted to the latter material in about 350). Some two hundred bronze pinakia have been found (fig. 12). They measure about 11 × 2 × 0.2 centimeters and are incised or punched with one of the ten letters from alpha to kappa

FIGURE 12. A fragment of a *pinakion* dating to the mid-fourth century. The inscription shows that it was issued to Demophanes of the deme Kephesia. American School of Classical Studies at Athens: Agora Excavations.

as well as with the juror's name, deme, and, sometimes, his patronymic.[17]

Athens' courts probably met between 175 and 225 days of the year. (The Athenian calendar was not organized around weekdays and weekends, but it nevertheless was not lacking in regularly scheduled holidays. There were some sixty annually celebrated festival days on which the courts and the Athenian council did not meet. Courts could be in session, however, during the eighty or so monthly festival days the Athenians celebrated each year. By contrast, there are about one hundred monthly festival days—that is, Saturdays and Sundays—in our own calendar. All told, the Attic year had about 195 ordinary working days.) The six thousand men who formed the state's jury pool were not required to appear for service every time the courts were in session, but they were entitled to. Those who did appear and were selected to serve on a case were paid three obols (a half drachma) for their trouble, a modest amount but enough to make the prospect of a day in court appealing for many. Because of this possibility of compensation, juries may have been composed of a disproportionately high number of Athens' poorer citizens as well as older men who were not capable of doing more physically demanding labor. Certainly Aristophanes portrays jurors as old and short of funds in his comedy *Wasps*. In the play, an old man who is addicted to jury service is eventually persuaded by his son to give up going to court all the time—the catch being that the old man will now judge cases at home involving the peccadilloes of the slaves and household pets. The chorus of the play is composed of old men who are likewise eager dicasts.[18]

When a juror did show up at court in the morning he and his fellow dicasts went through an elaborate procedure by which they were either rejected for service on that day or selected and distributed among different courtrooms. It is worth describing the procedure in detail to give a taste of the jurors' experience before the trial began—and the lengths to which the Athenians went to prevent judicial corruption. The procedure is described in detail in sections 63–66 of the *Constitution of Athens*.[19]

As we mentioned in Chapter 6, Athens' citizens were divided into ten geographically based tribes in accordance with which certain civic functions were organized. In particular, citizens who appeared for jury duty were divided into their tribes, and their selection and allotment to particular courtrooms was conducted by each tribe separately.

There were ten entrances into the court area, one for each tribe, and some number of individual courtrooms. We may perhaps imagine a courtyard or lobby area into which the tribal entrances led and which gave access to the courtrooms. It would not be necessary to use all of the rooms every day. Those that were to be used were randomly assigned a letter, starting with lambda (the eleventh letter of the alphabet), by which they would be designated for that day.

Jurors arriving at the court went to the entrance that corresponded to their tribe. At the entrance there were ten boxes, each marked with one of the first ten letters of the alphabet (alpha to kappa). Each juror put his pinakion—these tickets, it will be remembered, likewise had letters on them—into the box having the same letter. The boxes were then shaken by an official, and one man's name was drawn from each box. The men thus selected would act as "inserters" for their letter (alpha to kappa) for the remainder of the selection process.

At each tribal entrance there were also two *kleroteria*, or allotment machines (fig. 13). These were tall blocks, each having five columns of slots. Each column was labeled with one of the letters from alpha to kappa, the first five letters of the alphabet on one *kleroterion*, the second five on the other. Each inserter selected pinakia from the box designated by the letter on his own pinakion, and he inserted the tickets, in the order in which he drew them, into the corresponding column of slots on the

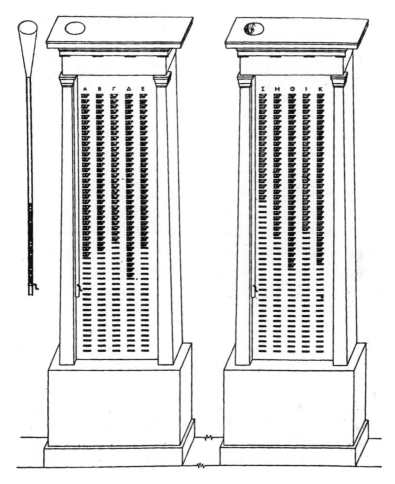

FIGURE 13. A reconstruction of two *kleroteria*, or allotment machines. American School of Classical Studies at Athens: Agora Excavations.

kleroteria, starting at the top. When all the pinakia were in-serted, some of the columns would naturally be longer than oth-ers. Probably any tickets in the longer columns that were below the length of the shortest column were withdrawn from the kleroteria and returned to their owners, who were dismissed for the day.[20]

Now, each of the ten tribes had to produce 10 percent of the total number of jurors needed for the day, or 5 percent from each tribal kleroterion. The pinakia that remained in the kleroteria were selected in groups of five, row by row, until the tribe's quota was met. In order to determine which rows of pinakia would be selected and which tickets returned at once to their owners, another complicated procedure was followed. On the side of each of the kleroteria there was a tube topped by a funnel and having a release mechanism at the bottom. A number of cubes were poured into the funnel, some white and some black, so that they dropped into the tube in random order. The number of white cubes used was equal to the number of rows of jurors that the kleroterion had to produce. The number of black cubes was equal to the total number of occupied rows in the kleroterion less the number of white cubes. Suppose, for example, that the tribe had to produce a hundred jurors for the day. (We do not know how the one odd juror who served on each trial was selected.) The men who had served as inserters would automatically become jurors, thus the two kleroteria had to produce ninety jurors, nine rows selected from each machine. If, say, fifteen rows of the kleroteria were filled, then nine white cubes and six black cubes were poured into the funnel. The cubes were released one by one from the bottom of the tube. If a white cube was released first, then the jurors whose pinakia were in the first row of the kleroterion were selected for service. A black cube indicated that the row under consideration was rejected. Each row was selected or rejected until nine white balls had been removed from the tube. The pinakia in the rejected rows were returned to their owners, who were dismissed, while the jurors whose rows had been selected moved on to another allotment procedure.

In order to find out in which courtroom he would serve a juror who had been selected by the kleroterion next drew a ball from an urn. The urn contained as many balls as the number of jurors the tribe had to produce that day. The balls were marked with letters, starting with lambda, that corresponded to the letters the courts had already been assigned. The number of balls with the letter omicron on them, for example, would have been equal to the number of jurors from each tribe that were required to serve in courtroom omicron. After drawing his lettered ball from the urn the juror showed it to an official, who took the juror's pinakion and put it in a box marked with the letter on the ball. The juror next showed the ball to an attendant, who gave him a colored staff. The color on the staff corresponded to the color that was painted over the door of the courtroom designated by the letter the juror had drawn from the urn. The juror took the colored staff and, still holding the ball he had drawn from the urn, went to the correspondingly colored courtroom. There he was given a ticket (not his pinakion) the purpose of which is not clear, but which may have indicated the section of the courtroom in which the juror was to sit. When all the jurors had come out the other end of this complex selection procedure, the trial proper—or its immediate antecedents, which we will consider in the next section—could begin.

In addition to minimizing the possibility of jury tampering, this delightfully complicated selection process ensured that every jury panel was composed of a cross section of the Athenian citizen population. Every tribe was represented in equal numbers, and even within tribes the sections designated by the letters alpha to kappa were equally represented. We should note also the astoundingly high level of participation in the process that a jury pool of six thousand citizens implies. In the fourth century the number of citizens eligible to serve as jurors—fully enfranchised men over the age of thirty—cannot have been much above twenty thousand. Thus some 30 percent of the eligible population served as jurors every year. And they served for an entire year. If they did not appear for the selection procedure every day the courts were in session, they must have done so at least a few times in the course of the year. Even in comparison with that minimal degree of participation, the onus of jury duty imposed nowadays on the citizens of modern democracies is trivial.[21]

COURTROOM PROCEDURE

When the jurors were seated there remained a bit more administrative work to do. It will be remembered that when a juror showed his lettered ball to the official, the official took the juror's pinakion and put it into a box marked with the same letter as the letter on the ball. When the jury selection process was complete, the boxes were brought to the courtrooms whose letters they shared. Each courtroom would thus have ten separate boxes, one from each tribe, each filled with the names of the jurors from that tribe who were sitting in the courtroom.

The magistrate who was to preside over the courtroom selected one pinakion from each of the ten boxes. (Readers should not imagine that the presiding magistrate played a role in the proceedings similar to that of a modern judge. The magistrate did not officiate during the trial, ruling on the admissibility of evidence, for example, or issuing instructions to the jury.) The ten men whose names were thus selected were made to perform certain tasks in connection with the trial—five would be in charge of the payment of the jurors at the end of the day, four would oversee the voting, and one would keep an eye on the water clock. (Note once again the Athenians' reliance not only on randomly selected jurors but also on amateurs. There was no large court staff ready—or trusted—to perform these jobs.) After the selection of these ten, the charges against the defendant were read out, the litigants swore an oath to stick to the point when making their speeches (a requirement that was regularly disregarded), and the trial began.[22]

The time that was given to private trials, dikai—and thus

the time given to the litigants to speak—varied according to the amount of money that was at issue in the case, but even the longest of these took no more than a few hours. Graphai, on the other hand, took a full day (the length of a "day" being determined by the length of the shortest day of the year, so about nine and a half hours). The day was divided into three equal parts, with roughly three hours being given to the prosecutor, who spoke first, and his synegoroi (if he used them), three given to the defendant and his synegoroi, and three for the jury selection and casting of ballots. In addition, if the trial was an agon timetos—one in which the penalty was not prescribed by law but would be determined by the jurors—then the third part of the day was given over also to the brief speeches the litigants made in proposing their penalties.[23]

The litigants' speeches were timed with a *klepsydra* or water clock (figs. 14, 15). The clock consisted of two vessels, one placed above the other. Each had a hole at its rim, to ensure that it would always fill to the same level, and a spout near the bottom through which, when it was not plugged, water would flow at a known rate. During the trial the upper vessel, having been filled to capacity, would be allowed to empty into the lower bowl, after which the position of the two vessels could quickly be reversed. This would be done repeatedly, as the litigants were given a number of measures of water—precisely how many depended on the type of trial in question—in which to make their presentations. Presumably the job of reversing the bowls was performed by the juror who had been assigned to the water clock at the beginning of the proceedings. It was his job also to stop the water at times by plugging up the hole. Litigants in private suits very frequently directed the juror at the water clock to "stop the water" while laws or depositions were read out by a secretary. (Apollodoros refers to the water clock himself in section 20 of his speech. He promises to provide the jurors with further details later in his speech about the men who pur-

FIGURE 14. A working model of the *klepsydra*, the water clock by
which lawcourt speeches were timed. American School of Classical
Studies at Athens: Agora Excavations.

chased Nikarete's prostitutes, "if you wish to hear and I have
surplus water.") The time taken in introducing such evidence
to the court was not counted against the time granted to the
litigants to speak in these shorter suits.[24]

By the time Theomnestos began to address the court at
Neaira's trial, the 501 jurors hearing the case had already undergone the selection procedure outside of the courtroom, and ten
of their number, one from each tribe, had been selected within
the court to perform odd jobs. The jurors were seated, still holding their colored staves, and they were ready to spend the next
few hours listening to the prosecution team of Theomnestos and

Apollodoros. The jurors would not necessarily have done so quietly. Lawcourt speeches were frequently interrupted by murmurs or shouts from the floor. The litigants themselves sometimes used the phenomenon of courtroom noise to their advantage, urging the jurors to tell one another about information relevant to the case, for example, or inviting them to inter-

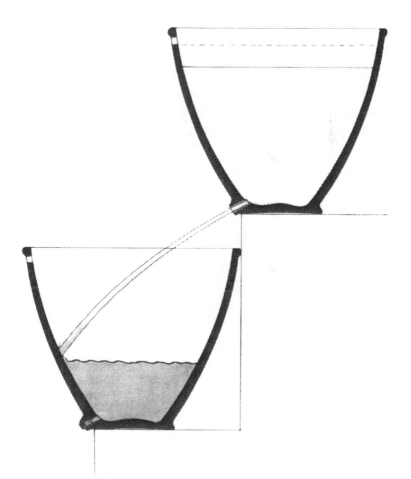

FIGURE 15. A drawing of two *klepsydrai*. American School of Classical Studies at Athens: Agora Excavations.

rupt or pose questions of their opponents when the latter ascended the speaker's platform. The trial, that is, was not a staid
affair, and the jurors hardly a passive audience.[25]

After hearing Apollodoros' speech for the prosecution, the
jurors sat for another three hours or so listening to Stephanos'
defense. Then, without any summing up by the presiding magistrate or formal deliberation among the jurors, the voting procedure began. The jurors rose and surrendered their colored staves
to the men who had been selected to superintend the vote. They
received in return two ballots, one for the prosecution and one
for the defense. These ballots were bronze disks that were
pierced by an axle. The axle was either hollow or solid, the former signifying a vote for the prosecution and the latter a vote
for the defense (figs. 16, 17). Jurors held the ballots between
their thumbs and forefingers in order to conceal the ends of the
axles, then cast their votes by dropping the appropriate ballot

FIGURE 16. A hollow ballot, for the prosecution, dating to the Hellenistic period. It is inscribed *psephos:demosia*, or "public ballot."
American School of Classical Studies at Athens: Agora Excavations.

FIGURE 17. A solid ballot, for the defense, dating to the late fourth century. American School of Classical Studies at Athens: Agora Excavations.

into a bronze amphora and discarding the other, which would not be counted, into a wooden amphora. The jurors were then given a bronze token, marked with a three, which they would exchange at the end of the day for their three-obol payment.[26]

It remained only for the votes to be counted. (In agones timetoi, if the first vote resulted in a guilty verdict, there followed a second vote in which the jurors decided between penalties proposed by the litigants. In Neaira's trial, because it was not an agon timetos, there would be no second vote.) The jurors who were in charge of the procedure poured the ballots from the bronze amphora onto a counting board that had as many holes in it as the number of ballots that had been cast. The ballots fell into the holes, making it easier to count them. After the votes had been tallied a herald announced the results, the case being decided by simple majority. The defendant rejoiced or lamented as appropriate, and the jurors themselves divided into tribes to receive their payment. (In private cases, of course, the jurors had more work to do before they were paid. They returned to their seats and would hear several more cases before the day was out.) The jurors who were overseeing this procedure read out the dicasts' names from the pinakia that had been collected before the trial. The jurors came forward as their names were read, handed in the tokens they had received after voting, and received in return their pinakia and three-obol payment, a small reward for a day spent making Athens' democracy work.

IX

NEAIRA'S

TRIAL

After some three hours spent haranguing the 501 jurors trying Neaira's case, Apollodoros' water clock ran dry for the last time. He yielded the floor to his enemy, Stephanos, who would speak in Neaira's defense. But how successful had the prosecutor's attack on Neaira been? Has Apollodoros convinced us, Neaira's modern jury, that the defendant was guilty of the offense with which she was charged?

THE PROSECUTION'S CASE

The moment he ascended the speaker's platform at Neaira's trial Apollodoros told the jurors what he intended to prove to them:

"Gentlemen of Athens, Theomnestos has told you what I suffered at Stephanos' hands that prompted me to come forward and accuse this woman Neaira; but I wish to prove this to you clearly, that Neaira is a foreigner and that she lives in marriage with Stephanos, contrary to the laws" (§16). Neaira stood accused of living in a marriage relationship with an Athenian citizen while being herself a foreigner, a union that was illegal under the law Apollodoros next has read out in court:

> First, then, the law will be read out to you in accordance with which Theomnestos brought this graphe, and in accordance with which this trial comes before you:
>
> THE LAW
> If a foreigner lives in marriage with a citizen woman by any manner or means, anyone of the Athenians who wishes and for whom it is legally possible may bring an indictment before the *thesmothetai* [six of the so-called nine archons; they presided over most graphai]. If he is convicted, he and his property will be sold, and a third part of it given to the prosecutor. The same punishment will apply if a foreign woman lives in marriage with a male citizen in the same way, and the man who lives in marriage with the convicted foreign woman will be fined 1,000 drachmas. (§16)

Given the charge, Apollodoros' assessment of what he needed to demonstrate—that Neaira was a foreigner and was living as Stephanos' wife—is of course right on the mark. But was he successful in making his case to the court?

Apollodoros begins at once on his proof of the first claim. He demonstrates that Neaira was a foreigner by providing a detailed description of her early life. He offers the testimony of witnesses who verify that Neaira was a prostitute in Nikarete's stable and that she managed later to buy her freedom, with the help of the Athenian Phrynion, from Eukrates and Timanorides of Corinth

(§§18–32). Apollodoros' lengthy account of Neaira's time with Phrynion and the latter's subsequent attempt to hale her into slavery, while longer than is strictly necessary, provides a further proof of Neaira's status: she was required at the time to provide sureties before the polemarch, one of Athens' nine archons and the official who supervised cases concerning metics (§§33–48).[1]

In section 49 of his speech Apollodoros sums up his argument to that point: "I show you in my speech, and testimony has been given, that Neaira was from the beginning a slave, and she was sold twice, and she worked with her body as a hetaira, and she ran away from Phyrnion to Megara, and she went before the polemarch and provided sureties as a foreigner." We may indeed agree that Apollodoros has established beyond any reasonable doubt that Neaira was not an Athenian citizen. It is more proof, perhaps, than was necessary, for there is no indication in Apollodoros' speech—and he does refer to the arguments to be expected from the defense (§§118–119)—that Stephanos had any intention of alleging that Neaira was *not* a foreigner.

Apollodoros, however, has even more evidence to offer on the question. He discusses Phano's checkered history at great length in his speech (§§50–87), claiming that Stephanos and others gave proof by their actions that Phano was an alien. (And Phano's citizenship status, according to Apollodoros, was a reflection of Neaira's status.) In the wake of Phano's unhappy marriage to Phrastor, for example, both Stephanos and Phrastor, according to Apollodoros, acted as if Phano was a foreigner:[2]

I show you clearly that even those who are most closely related to this woman Neaira have given testimony that she is an alien, both Stephanos here, who now has her and lives in marriage with her, and Phrastor, who married her daughter—Stephanos when he did not wish to contend in court on behalf of Neaira's daughter, after he was indicted before the thesmothetai by Phrastor on the charge that he had betrothed to Phrastor, an Athenian, the daughter of a foreign woman, and when he gave up his claim to the dowry and did not get it back; and Phrastor when he threw out the daughter of this Neaira after he had married her, when he learned that she was not the daughter of Stephanos, and he did not give back the dowry; later too, when he was persuaded—because of his illness and childlessness and his animosity toward his relatives—to acknowledge his son, and when he introduced the boy to his fellow gennetai but was unwilling to swear an oath when the gennetai rejected the boy and challenged him to swear; and later yet when he married a citizen woman according to the law; for these actions, which are quite clear, have given great proofs against them, that Neaira here is a foreigner. (§§62–63)[3]

Apollodoros likewise adduces as proof that Phano was an alien both Stephanos' decision to settle out of court with Epainetos, after the latter was caught in flagrante delicto with Phano (§§64–71), and Theogenes' decision to divorce Phano after the Areopagos Council's inquiry into her background (§§72–87). These arguments, of course, assume that Phano is Neaira's daughter, a claim which may be true but is not adequately proved in the speech.

Apollodoros thus spends seventy sections of his 126-section speech addressing the question of Neaira's status as an alien, a point which the defense was probably not about to contest and which was, at any rate, adequately addressed by Apollodoros after a mere fifteen sections. We can be forgiven for thinking that the prosecutor, in dwelling on the citizenship question, was playing to his strengths: he did not have much ammunition when it came to proving his second claim, that Neaira was living in a marriage relationship with Stephanos.

Apollodoros, in fact, put off his discussion of that question even further. Sections 88–93 of the speech are a discussion of the Athenians' procedure for enfranchising aliens. In sections 94–106 Apollodoros digresses on the mass enfranchisement after 427 of the Plataeans, Athens' stalwart allies. And sections 107–117 are given over to various digressions and rants against Neaira, as, for example, this litany of abuse in section 108:

> Where did she not work with her body, or where did she not go for her daily wage? Was she not in all the Peloponnese, and in Thessaly and Magnesia with Simos of Larissa and Eurydamas the son of Medeios, in Chios and in most of Ionia accompanying Sotadas of Crete, hired out by Nikarete when she was still that woman's slave? What do you think a woman does who is under the control of others and who follows whoever gives her money? Doesn't she service in every kind of pleasure those who make use of her? So a woman who is known by all clearly to be of such a sort, who has made a circuit of the earth, making her living from three holes, will you vote that she is a citizen?[4]

Apollodoros finally turns, in the last few minutes of his speech (§118–125), to a discussion of the type of relationship Neaira and Stephanos shared. It is at this point that he claims, as we have seen already in Chapter 3, that Stephanos' behavior toward the children—the fact that he has acted as if they were Athenian citizens—proves that he has been living in a marriage relationship with Neaira. (Apollodoros' lengthy discussion of Phano's marriages earlier in his speech provides the background necessary for him to make this claim.) We have seen that this line of argument is not convincing. Apollodoros fails to prove that the children in question were in fact born to Neaira and were not Stephanos' offspring by a citizen wife, the argument the defense is ready to advance (§119). If the children were not Neaira's, and in particular if they were not the product of Stephanos' union with her, then Stephanos' behavior toward them has nothing to tell us about the nature of his relationship with the aging courtesan he happened to live with.

Apollodoros' speech is poorly organized and his arguments are frequently irrelevant. He leaves to the very end of his discussion the more important of the two proofs he promised the jurors in the first sentence of his speech. When Apollodoros finally does address the topic of Stephanos' relationship with Neaira, the evidence he adduces as proof that the two are living in a marriage relationship is not persuasive. Presented with ballots ourselves, we jurors—with our modern sensibilities, and with more time to consider Neaira's guilt or innocence than her historical jurors had—must in good conscience drop solid ballots into the bronze amphora: the defendant was *not*, we must imagine, guilty as charged.

COUNTING THE BALLOTS

But before we turn our backs on the day's litigation and run off to surrender our staves and collect our three-obol payment, we should consider the rest of the ballots that were caught in the holes of the reckoning board after Neaira's trial. Were the real dicasts—the Athenians who sat shoulder to shoulder one long day two and a half millennia ago and heard Apollodoros himself deliver in his booming voice the words we have read—likewise struck by the prosecutor's failure to provide convincing proof of his charge?

As is true of nearly all the trials from which one or more of the litigants' speeches have survived, we do not know the outcome of this lawsuit. Nor can we conclude, because of the weakness of Apollodoros' case, that the defendant is likely to have prevailed. Stephanos, for all we know, presented an even weaker case when he spoke in Neaira's defense. Unfortunately we do not have his speech from the trial to contrast with Apollodoros'. More to the point, the jurors trying the case, the men whose ballots plunked to the bottom of the bronze amphora that day, may not have made their decision based only on the facts of the case.

When the panel of six thousand jurors was selected for service at the beginning of each year, the dicasts swore an oath affirming that they would, among other things, give their verdict in any given trial based only on the charges brought by the prosecution. In theory, then, the jurors trying Neaira's case were bound to weed out the facts from Apollodoros' maze of rhetoric and cast their ballots accordingly. But there was no presiding judge in an Athenian courtroom to issue instructions about what jurors could or could not consider when making their judgment. There was no period of deliberation with their fellow dicasts during which jurors might be required to defend their votes by reference to the litigants' arguments. The jurors were in fact free to decide the case in accordance with any considerations they fancied. They might penalize Apollodoros, for example, for being wealthy or boorish or the son of a former slave. Or they might come to a decision based not on the defendant's guilt or innocence but on the conduct of the litigants in the larger feud of which Neaira's trial was a part.[5]

Litigants, meanwhile, tried to sway juries in their favor not only through a recitation of the facts of the case, but also by appealing to their audience's emotions and biases. Not for nothing did Apollodoros include in his speech a lengthy digression on the Athenians' enfranchisement of the Plataeans, the only Greeks who had fought alongside the Athenians at Marathon in 490 (§§94–106). The digression does allow the prosecutor to make a point about Athens' enfranchisement standards. But, perhaps more important, it serves also as an appeal to the jurors' patriotism. Stephanos, for his part, is likely to have injected into his speech his own appeals to the jurors' prejudices. He may, for example, have tried to undermine Apollodoros' influence on the jury by stressing his opponent's excessive litigiousness, or he may have attempted to use Apollodoros' servile origins against him. The victory in this contest will not necessarily have gone to the litigant whose case was strongest. It may have gone instead to the speaker who was most adept at playing to the jurors' sensibilities. In the case of Theomnestos v. Neaira, we will probably never know who the more persuasive speaker was.

We know nothing whatever of Apollodoros' history after the trial of Neaira. His well-documented and litigious life ends for us in this last thrust at his sparring partner Stephanos. As for Neaira herself, who was so often at the command of others in her lifetime, let us hope the jurors' verdict left her free to return to her life with Stephanos—and free, perhaps, to give him hell for involving her in such a mess in the first place.[6]

NOTES

CHAPTER 1. NIKARETE'S BROTHEL

1. Throughout this book I refer to Apollodoros as the prosecutor of Neaira, but this is a kind of shorthand. The charges against Neaira were in fact brought by Theomnestos, Apollodoros' relative by marriage. See further Chapter 8.

2. Carey (1992, 2–3) suggests that Neaira was born sometime between 400 and 395. On the prominence of prostitutes in Corinth see, for example, Athenaeus, *Dinner-sophists* 13.573c–574d. Like Corinth, the Greek island of Lesbos in the northeast Aegean gave its name to a sexual act: *lesbiazein* meant "to fellate," a practice which the Lesbians were thought to have invented (see Henderson 1975, 175 and 183–184). For a modern parallel of these geographically inspired terms compare our own relatively tame "French kiss." Death owing to exposure was a common enough fate for Greek infants, and particularly for females. See Wilkinson 1978, 32–38; Pomeroy 1983; Todd 1993, 182 n. 27 and 184–185 n. 32.

3. For Anteia see Athenaeus, *Dinner-sophists* 13.567c, 13.586e; Patteson 1978, 48–49; Carey 1992, 94–95; Kapparis 1999, 44 and 208–209. Philetairos' remark is preserved at Athenaeus, *Dinner-sophists* 13.587e (= Philetaerus 9 K-A).

4. On those message-bearing sandals see Clement of Alexandria, *Tutor* 2.11.116, with Navarre 1904, 1828. (I am grateful to Alfred Kriman and Ulrich Schmitzer for locating this anecdote, and to Diana Wright for alerting me to a passage in Mary Renault's novel *The Last of the Wine* in which the sandals figure.) On the variety of prostitutes

available in modern societies cf. Kilmer 1993, 167 n. 101. On the difficulty of separating Greek prostitutes into distinct types see Kurke 1997, 108–109. See Garlan (1988, 45–53) on the origin of slaves. On the attire of prostitutes cf. Aristophanes, *Assemblywomen* 878–879, with Ussher 1973, 195; Lucian, *The Hall* 7, *Dialogues of the Courtesans* 297, *Loves* 39, *The Double Indictment* 31; Clement of Alexandria, *Tutor* 3.2.5; Navarre 1904, 1831–1832.

   My discussion in this section owes much to chapters 3 and 4 of James Davidson's *Courtesans and Fishcakes*. Interested readers are urged to consult his book for further information about Greek prostitution. See also Kapparis 1999, 4–8.

5. Lycurgus, *Against Leokrates* 39–40. For Xenarchos see Athenaeus, *Dinner-sophists* 13.569b = Xenarchus 4 K-A. On prostitutes beckoning from their brothels see Graham 1998, 23–32. Prostitutes, incidentally, continue to beckon men from windows to this day. In Walletjes, the infamous red-light district of Amsterdam, scarcely clad working girls eye prospective customers from behind plate-glass windows, where they sit displaying themselves like "female-shaped pieces of meat." (The phrase is Nick Middleton's, from *Travels as a Brussels Scout*. I owe this reference to Amsterdam's red-light district to my husband, for whose familiarity with Dutch prostitution I am, I suppose, grateful.)

6. See Loomis (1998, chap. 14), however, for the impossibility of defining a "standard Athenian wage." In the late fifth century, skilled workers and laborers employed in the construction of the Erechtheion on the Acropolis were paid between one and one and a half drachmas per day (Loomis, 105–107). At the end of the fourth century, skilled workers employed at a building project in the deme Eleusis earned between one and a quarter and two and a half drachmas daily (Loomis, 111–113). Citizens also received pay for public duties, a drachma for attending a regular meeting of the assembly and a half drachma, or three obols, for a day of jury service. Loomis (1998, chap. 9) and Davidson (1997, 194–200) collect evidence for the prices charged by various prostitutes. See also Starr 1978, 409 and n. 33.

   On sexual positions see Davidson 1997, 118 and 196. For the numerous positions in which heterosexual couples are depicted on red-figure vases, see Kilmer 1993, 33–59 and 73–75. (Various types of copulation *a tergo* are the most frequently represented.) On the desirability of the "racehorse" position cf. the story told by Athenaeus at *Dinner-sophists* 13.581c-f (= Gow 1965, frag. 17 lines 349–375).

7. Xenophon, *Symposium* 2.1–2. For an introduction to the Greek symposium see Davidson 1997, 43–49.
8. Aristophanes, *Wasps* 1345–1346. Athenaeus, *Dinner-sophists* 13.607e.
9. [Aristotle], *Constitution of Athens* 50.2.
10. Cf. Loomis 1998, 93–94 and 173. The Hyperides passage is 4 *For Euxenippos* 3, with which see Whitehead 2000, 178–179. See also Starr 1978, 406–407.
11. See Menander, *The Samian Girl* 392–396; Davidson 1997, 197–198. For the witty repartee of hetairai see book 13 of Athenaeus' *Dinner-sophists*. Greek hetairai have sometimes been compared to Japanese geisha, professional entertainers whose work likewise entailed some measure of sexual activity. Readers may enjoy Arthur Golden's *Memoirs of a Geisha*, which describes how a class of *hetaira*-like women functioned in early twentieth-century Japanese society.
12. Xenophon, *Memoirs of Socrates* 3.11.4. See Davidson (1997, 120–127 and 201–205) on the strategies hetairai adopted to obscure the nature of their business. Cf. Cohen (1998, 116–117) on the similar behavior of Helen Jewett, a nineteenth-century prostitute.
13. The same attitude toward a man's resort to brothels was allegedly expressed by the Roman statesman Cato. See Krenkel 1988, 1295. Although prostitution was legal in Athens, Athenian *males* who prostituted themselves were no longer free to exercise their civic rights. See Harrison 1968, 37–38; Hansen 1976a, 74; Cohen 1991, 176. For the taxation of prostitutes see Aeschines, *Against Timarchos* 119; Dover 1978, 30. On Greek attitudes toward expenditure on women and boys see Dover 1984, 147–148; Davidson 1997, 194–195.
14. On the possibility of bedding one's slaves cf. Davidson 1997, 99.
15. The management of a Greek home was an important and demanding job. See Hunter (1994, 34–35) for an excellent description of an ancient woman's responsibilities. On the position of Spartan women see, for example, Xenophon, *The Politeia of the Spartans* 1.4–10; Aristotle, *Politics* 1269b–1270b; Cartledge 1981; Lefkowitz 1983, 55. On the segregation of Greek women generally, which is not to be understood as implying seclusion from society, see, for example, Dover 1974, 209–213; 1984; Walker 1983; Cohen 1991, 146–154; Nevett 1995; Morris 1998, 213–218; Kapparis 1999, 217–221.

16. The conventional date of the trial is between 343 and 340 (see Kapparis 1999, 28), though Apollodoros may in fact have prosecuted Neaira any time between 348 and 339. See Wallace (2000, 591), who argues for a date earlier rather than later in the 340s.
17. For Euxitheos' mother see Demosthenes 57 *Against Euboulides* 34.
18. Athenaeus *Dinner-sophists* 569b = Xenarchus 4 K-A.
19. On the comic aspects of Lysias' story see Porter (1997), who suggests that Lysias' speech was in fact a "particularly sophisticated form of practical rhetorical exercise—a fictional speech based upon a fictional case." On adultery see Cohen 1991, 98–170; Patterson 1998, chapters 4–5.
20. I have given a description of the Greater Mysteries, held annually in September or October. To qualify for initiation into these rites, one had first to be initiated into the Lesser Mysteries, a ceremony that was performed in late February. Kapparis (1999, 212) suggests that Apollodoros is referring to this preliminary initiation rather than to the Greater Mysteries. We simply cannot know from the text, however, which of the ceremonies is meant. On the Mysteries generally see Parke 1977, 55–72. Metaneira's status as a non-Athenian and a prostitute was not an impediment to her participation in the ceremony. Initiation into the Mysteries was open to any Greek, slave or free, male or female, who could pay for the privilege and was not contaminated, for example, by bloodguilt. Lysias himself, as we will see, was not a citizen of Athens but only an alien resident in the city.
21. On Neaira's age see Kapparis 1999, 215. Greek men, and particularly wealthy ones, had abundant opportunity to engage in extramarital sexual relationships, and it is reasonable to assume that many of them, if not all, availed themselves of the possibilities their society offered. (See further Dover 1974, 210; Davidson 1997, 137–138.) But for a married man to introduce prostitutes into his home was an insult to his wife, so offensive that it might prompt her to seek divorce. On divorce in Athens see Andocides 4 *Against Alcibiades* 14; Plutarch, *Alcibiades* 8; Harrison 1968, 38–44; Cohn-Haft 1995; Kapparis 1999, 212–213 and 271–272.
22. Plato, *Republic* 328b–c. It is not clear how long before Polemarchos' death this scene is supposed to have occurred, as there are obstacles to determining the dramatic date of the *Republic*. Years between 424 and 408 have been proposed. See Nails 1998, 383–396.
23. For the number of those executed by the Thirty see Krentz 1982,

79 and n. 30. On the tyrants' actions see for example Lysias 25 *Defense Against a Charge of Subverting the Democracy* 19, and [Aristotle], *Constitution of Athens* 35.3. On sycophancy see further Chapter 4. The Athenians had a penchant for naming boards of officials after the number of men serving on the board. In addition to the Thirty, there were the Ten (who held power briefly in Athens after the Thirty were deposed), the Eleven (who supervised the prison), the Forty (who often presided over the lawcourts), and the Five Hundred (councilors who were responsible for arranging the agenda of the democratic assembly).

24. Lysias 12 *Against Eratosthenes* 7–17. Execution by hemlock in Athens is familiar to us from the example of Socrates, who was forced to quaff the stuff in 399. But death by hemlock poisoning was not in fact the relatively pleasant affair Plato describes in his account of Socrates' death in the *Phaedo*—numbness starting at the feet and gradually moving upward to the heart. For a discussion of the effects of hemlock poisoning on the body see Gill 1973. The Eratosthenes mentioned here is almost certainly not the man whose death is discussed in Lysias' *On the Murder of Eratosthenes*. On the question see most recently Todd 2000, 15.

25. Lysias 12 *Against Eratosthenes* 19–20.

26. Our sources disagree about the numbers of mercenaries and shields Lysias provided. See Krentz 1982, 73 and n. 11. For the role of Thrasyboulos in the restoration of the democracy see Buck 1998, 71–93. Mary Renault breathes life into this ugly period of Athens' history in her novel *The Last of the Wine*.

27. For an introduction to Lysias' style and work, see Edwards 1999, 3–8. S. C. Todd has provided a translation of the speeches, part of the Oratory of Classical Greece series. Regarding the date at which Lysias took up his new career: all but one of the dateable speeches in the Lysianic corpus belong to the period between 403 and roughly 380. Lysias 20 *For Polystratos* must be dated to 410 or 409, but the authorship of this speech has been questioned. See Dover 1968b, 44, 56; Todd 2000, 217.

28. The date of Lysias' birth is disputed. According to the ancient tradition, he was born in 459, but some scholars argue for a date in the 440s. See especially Dover 1968a, 34–46. In dating these events I have followed Carey 1992, 2–3.

29. For the date of Neaira's visit to Athens, see Kapparis 1999, 217. On the Panathenaia see Parke 1977, 35–50.

30. For the career of Simos see Martin 1985, 255–260.
31. Demosthenes 27 *Against Aphobos I* 9. Kapparis 1999, 227–228: "Neaira was sold at the top average price for a courtesan."
32. On sexual positions and handbooks see Davidson 1997, 117–118; cf. Parker 1992; Kilmer 1993, 74–75. See Kurke (1997, 140–141) for late evidence on what constituted proper hetairic behavior at symposia, a further subject in which Nikarete's prostitutes may have needed instruction. On the education of hetairai see Kapparis 1999, 6.
33. Isaeus 3 *On the Estate of Pyrrhus* 13. Lysias 1 *On the Murder of Eratosthenes* 23.
34. Lysias 3 *Against Simon* 6.
35. For the women mentioned see Isaeus 2 *On the Estate of Menekles* 18; Isaeus 6 *On the Estate of Philoktemon* 10; Demosthenes 40 *Against Boiotos II* 6. On the Athenians' reticence about naming women see Schaps 1977. He cites (328–329) three passages only in which litigants referred to living, reputable women by name, in each case because the full identification of the woman was necessary for the speaker's prosecution of the case.
36. On Onetor's sister see Schaps 1977, 326.

CHAPTER 2. OWNERS AND OTHER LOVERS

1. The quote is from Kapparis 1999, 214–215; cf. Carey 1992. Kapparis 1999, 228, suggests that Neaira was sold to Timanoridas and Eukrates in 376. Most Greek girls married for the first time when they were between fourteen and nineteen. See Lacey 1968, 71–72, 106–107, and 162–163; Pomeroy 1975, 64; Just 1989, 151; Kapparis 1999, 214.
2. Lysias 4 *On a Premeditated Wounding* 8, 12, 16.
3. For the duration of the partners' ownership of Neaira see Kapparis 1999, 228.
4. On brothels see Davidson 1997, 83–91; Kapparis 1999, 228–229. Keuls (1985, 156) writes: "We have no knowledge of the conditions prevailing in the brothels of Corinth and Athens, but there is no reason to assume that they were any more commodious than the dark and stinking holes in which Roman whores practiced their trade, and of which Roman authors have left us descriptions."
5. On the avarice of brothel-keepers see Carey 1992, 101; Kapparis 1999, 229.

6. Carey 1992, 102.
7. On conditional manumission see Harrison 1968, 184; Patteson 1978, 68; Garlan 1988, 77–79; Carey 1992, 102; Kapparis 1999, 233.
8. Cf. Patteson 1978, 63. The quote is from Carey 1992, 102.
9. Athenaeus, *Dinner-sophists* 13.570c–d = Epicrates 3 K-A. See Keuls (1985, 200–203) on aging prostitutes.
10. On communication by personal letter, which was relatively uncommon, see Lewis 1996, 142–152.
11. On the terms of the agreement between Neaira and her benefactors see Patteson 1978, 64–65; Millett 1991, 158; Cohen 1992, 207–215; Kapparis 1999, 231–232. See further also Chapter 4.
12. Phrynion himself did not necessarily live in Paiania, however: deme membership was hereditary, and it was possible to move one's residence from one deme to another. See the maps in Traill (1975) or Whitehead (1986b, xxiii) for what is known of the location of the demes within Attica. For an introduction to the political organization of Attica see Hansen 1991, 46–48 and 101–106.
13. On public intercourse see Dover 1974, 206. Certainly Xenophon found it odd that one of the tribes he and his fellow Greeks encountered in Persia in the early fourth century practiced public copulation (*The Persian Expedition* 5.4.33–34). Lucian, too, writing in the second century A.D., similarly suggests that among (living) Greeks of his day, having sex in front of an audience was not the done thing (*True Histories* 2.19).
14. See Develin (1989, Index I no. 556) for a précis of Chabrias' career. He lists in the Index fifteen generalships known for Chabrias, but three of these (for 379, 371, and 368) are marked as questionable in the text. Demosthenes 20 *Against Leptines* 75–78 gives an account of Chabrias' successes.
15. Keuls (1985, 182) sees the incident at Chabrias' house as an act of multiple rape, but it is not clear to me that the guests' (and slaves') use of Neaira constituted that offense.
16. See Munn (1993, 155–161) on Chabrias' Boeotian campaign. For a brief account of the Boeotian War, see Hamilton 1997, 78–81.
17. On the Battle of Leuctra see Anderson 1970, 192–220; Sage 1996, 137–140; Hamilton 1997, 81–86. On the shortage of manpower in Sparta see Cartledge 1987, 37–43 and 179.

CHAPTER 3. SONS AND CITIZENSHIP IN ANCIENT ATHENS

1. Kapparis (1999, 244–245) makes a good case for Stephanos' visit with Neaira in Megara being a relatively lengthy one.
2. Carey (1992, 112) suggests that "Phano," insofar as it is etymologically connected with the verb *phainein*, meaning "to show, display," was an inappropriate nickname for a respectable woman, but was suitable for a hetaira. In other words, it may have been a "Pussy Galore" sort of name, suggestive enough to get a man's attention. Kapparis (1999, 266), however, argues that "names implying visibility and brightness" did not carry this sense and were sufficiently dignified for use by citizen women: Socrates' mother, for example, was a perfectly respectable woman by the name of Phainarete. The reason for Phano's name change, Kapparis suggests, was rather to deemphasize the name "Strybele," which is etymologically connected with the verb *strephesthai* ("to turn about; be engaged in"), and which, other scholars have argued, suggested servility: if it *did* suggest servility, Kapparis writes, "Apollodoros implies that Stephanos and Neaira substituted the servile name of the woman with a dignified one, in order to disguise her origin." On nicknames and hetairai, see also Cox 1998, 175–177.
3. On contraceptives and abortifacients see Krenkel 1988, 1294–1295; Riddle 1992, 16–19 and 74–82. If these methods of birth control proved ineffectual, infanticide remained a less attractive (but legal) option for responding to a pregnancy. See Harrison 1968, 71; Pomeroy 1983; Patterson 1985, 103–123; Riddle 1992, 10–11. See Riddle (1992, 143) also on the secrets said to have been employed by prostitutes in the Roman period to avoid or terminate pregnancies.
4. On enrollment in the phratry see Just 1989, 56–62; Hansen 1991, 46 and 96; Carey 1992, 105; Todd 1993, 179; Kapparis 1999, 192–193. On the deme register see MacDowell 1978, 69; Hansen 1991, 88–89 and 104.
5. On the enfranchisement of aliens see MacDowell 1978, 70–73. For the sources for Pericles' citizenship law of 451, which restricted citizenship to the offspring of two citizen parents, see Develin 1989, 80. Pericles' law seems not to have been observed for a time during the Peloponnesian War. It was reinstated in 403, however, and in the 380s a stricter law governing citizenship was introduced. See Kapparis 1999, 199–202.
6. Cf. Trevett 1992, 100; Patteson 1978, 14; Patterson 1991.

7. In §122 Apollodoros continues: "We have prostitutes for the sake of pleasure, mistresses for the daily service of our bodies, and wives for the purpose of begetting legitimate children and in order to have a trustworthy guardian of our households." His tripartite categorization has been much discussed by scholars interested in the role of women in Athenian society. See, for example, Cantarella 1987, 48–51; Davidson 1997, 73 with 326 n. 1. For an overview of scholarship on women in antiquity see Katz 1994.

8. Carey (1992, 11) is more precise: Stephanos' treatment of the children, even if they were his by Neaira, would reflect on his relationship with Neaira only if he passed them off as the legitimate product of his union *with her* (and not as his by a citizen wife). Otherwise his action is illegal, but it does not constitute proof that Neaira was guilty of living with Stephanos as his wife.

9. The children are referred to for the first time in §13 of the speech, however, where Theomnestos, Apollodoros' fellow prosecutor, summarizes the arguments that will be made by the prosecution.

10. Harrison 1971, 205–207; MacDowell 1978, 69. See Scafuro (1994) for a discussion of the Athenians' use of witnesses to prove citizenship. On the amphidromia see Garland 1990, 93–95.

11. Demosthenes 30 *Against Onetor I* 37.

12. On torture and slave testimony see Harrison 1971, 147–150; MacDowell 1978, 245–247; Garlan 1988, 42–43; Hansen 1991, 201; DuBois 1991, 35–38; Hunter 1994, 70–94 and 133–134; Mirhady 1996; Thur 1996; Kapparis 1999, 426–427.

13. Aristophanes, *Frogs* 612–626.

14. On the sacred olives see MacDowell 1978, 135; Todd 1993, 307–308; Todd 2000, 77–79; Hanson 1998, 236–237.

15. Lysias 7 *On the Olive Stump* 34–35.

16. A text purporting to be the challenge Apollodoros issued appears in his speech at §124, but it may be a later interpolation. For discussion see Kapparis 1999, 431–436. Carey (1992, 149–150) and Trevett (1992, 190–191) believe the preserved document is authentic. The challenge preserved in the text, at any rate, prescribes that Neaira be enslaved and the children declared aliens in the event that she is shown to be their mother. Whether the text is genuine or not, the prescribed punishment is credible, since it corresponds well to the penalties that attended conviction in court for the offense Neaira is charged with (§16).

17. Antiphon 5 *On the Murder of Herodes* 31–32. See Hunter (1994, 90–

91) for a discussion of the reasons one might refuse an opponent's challenge. On this passage see Kapparis 1999, 39–40.

18. Apollodoros tends to write long sentences, piling clauses on top of one another. My seventy-eight-word sentence above translates a sixty-two-word sentence in the original Greek of §125. The sentence is on the long side even for Apollodoros. See Trevett 1992, 63–64 and 106–107. According to his calculations, the average sentence in the *Against Neaira* contains about thirty words (273 sentences total and 8,195 words in the speech), compared with 21.6, for example, in Apollodoros' *Against Stephanos II* ([Demosthenes] 46).

19. On Apollodoros' anticipation of his opponent's arguments see Carey 1992, 146.

CHAPTER 4. STEPHANOS, BREADWINNER AND CHAMPION

1. On house prices see Kapparis 1999, 247. For Dorotheos' trierarchies see Carey 1992, 106; Davies 1971, 174.

2. Three thousand drachmas seems to have been at least an average-sized dowry, not the contribution of an impoverished father (or pseudo-father). See Carey 1992, 112; Kapparis 1999, 268–269.

3. For the possibility of having friends address the court in one's stead (or support), see Chapter 8.

4. On sycophancy see, e.g., MacDowell 1978, 62–66; Harvey 1990; Osborne 1990; Todd 1993, 92–94; Christ 1998, 48–71.

5. For Kallistratos see Sealey 1956.

6. On moicheia see, in general, Harrison 1968, 32–36; MacDowell 1978, 124–125; Todd 1993, 276–279. Cohen (1991, 99–109) argues that moicheia referred only to sexual relations with married women or concubines. See Kapparis (1999, 295–297) for bibliography on the question. On concubinage see Kapparis 1999, 8–13.

7. Demosthenes 23 *Against Aristokrates* 55. Lysias 1 *On the Murder of Eratosthenes* 17, 26. The formality of Euphiletos' quoted speech has sounded artificial to some, but see Bers 1997, 146–147: "But this does not prove anything, for at moments of excitement, clichés rise to the lips, especially if the words are recognized as 'performative.'"

8. Aristophanes, *Clouds* 1079–1085. Carey 1983, 53. Athenaeus, *Dinner-sophists* 13.569c–d = Xenarchus 4 K-A. On "radishing" see also Dover 1978, 105–106; Cohen 1985; Roy 1991; Carey 1993; Kap-

paris 1996. On radish types see Dover 1968a, 217, with Theophrastus, *History of Plants* 7.4.2. The likeliest candidate is perhaps the Corinthian variety of radish mentioned by Theophrastus. On female depilation see Slater 1968, 12–13; Kilmer 1982; Kilmer 1993, 133–141, 151–154.

9. Kapparis 1996, 70, 77.
10. On extorting money from moichoi see Cohen 1991, 127–130; Davidson 1997, 199–200.
11. On the date of the *Huntress* see Breitenbach 1908, 122–125.
12. See Harrison 1968, 178–179 and 221; MacDowell 1978, 80; Patteson 1978, 64–65 and 72–73; Carey 1992, 107–108; Kapparis 1999, 248–250.
13. Harrison 1968, 178–179; Patteson 1978, 72–73; MacDowell 1978, 76.
14. On public arbitrators see [Aristotle], *Constitution of Athens* 53.4. For private arbitration see Harrison 1971, 64–66; MacDowell 1978, 203–206; Todd 1993, 123–125; Hunter 1994, 55–62; Scafuro 1997, chap. 3; Kapparis 1999, 258–259.
15. The text I have translated as "for equal periods in alternation" literally reads "day for day," which suggests that Neaira was to be passed back and forth between the disputants on a daily basis. At §47, however, in what purports to be the text of the arbitrators' actual decision (as opposed to Apollodoros' paraphrase of it in §46) but which may be a later re-creation, we are told that "each would make use of Neaira for an equal number of days in the month." This suggests that they were exchanging Neaira at a less frenetic rate, half a month spent with her and half a month without, for example. On the face of it, this seems a more workable arrangement. Whatever the specifics, however, it is clear that the arbitrators were suggesting that Neaira be used alternately by the disputants for roughly equal periods of time.

CHAPTER 5. PHANO'S FIRST MARRIAGE

1. If Phano was born while Neaira was in Megara (whether she was in fact Neaira's daughter or was born to Stephanos by a citizen wife during roughly the same period), and if she was between fourteen and nineteen when she married Phrastor, the marriage should be dated between 358 and 353.
2. Tiresias, more than anyone, was in a position to know about the

relative libidinousness of men and women: according to one version of the myth, he had spent seven years of his life as a woman, changed in his sex as a penalty for having disturbed two copulating snakes. For the story see Apollodorus, *Library* 3.6.7, and Ovid, *Metamorphoses* 3.316–338. Cf. also Aristotle, *Politics* 1335a, and Aristophanes, *Lysistrata* 133–136. On marriage ages see Lacey 1968, 71–72, 106–107, and 162–163; Pomeroy 1975, 64; Just 1989, 146 and 151.

3. On Phano's likely fidelity see Kapparis 1999, 269–270.

4. For dowries see Harrison 1968, 45–60; Lacey 1968, 109–110; MacDowell 1978, 87–89; Just 1989, 72–75; Kapparis 1999, 273–274.

5. On the distinction between a suit for maintenance (*dike sitou*) and a suit for the dowry (*dike proikos*) see, for example, Kapparis 1999, 273: an unsuccessful defendant in a dike proikos was required to return the entire dowry at once, while a husband who lost a dike sitou could take his time repaying the dowry, but he would pay a high rate of interest on it (18 percent, whereas 12 percent was a more common rate for loans) until the entire sum was returned.

6. The text of what is purportedly the deposition given by Phrastor at Neaira's trial has been preserved in the speech (§54), although it may not be authentic (for discussion see Carey 1992, 114–115; Kapparis 1999, 276–277). The document gives a different order to these events: (1) Phrastor initiated an indictment against Stephanos for having given Neaira's daughter to him in marriage, (2) he threw Phano out of the house, and (3) Stephanos then brought a countersuit against Phrastor for retaining the dowry. This order of events would militate against the explanation for Phrastor's suit I have adopted in the narrative (that Phrastor's indictment was prompted by Stephanos' suit rather than his own indignation), and it would make it more likely that Phrastor was suing for cause— that is, that Phano was indeed an alien—rather than out of anger. That said, apart from any technical questions about its authenticity, the order of events as presented in the deposition makes Phrastor's actions hard to understand. Why would he have brought charges against Stephanos over Phano's status while retaining the dowry, which rendered him vulnerable to a suit for maintenance he was virtually guaranteed to lose? Apollodoros' presentation of the events in his narrative makes more sense of the actions and reactions of the two disputants.

7. On the strategy Phrastor adopted of threatening a lawsuit in response to charges brought against himself, a move which was tanta-

mount to "an invitation to settle out of court," see Scafuro 1997, 72–75. For a definition of atimia see Hansen 1976a, 55–56.

8. For the introduction of girls to phratries see Lambert 1993, 36–37 and 178–181. On the indirect proofs of a woman's citizenship status see also Gould 1980, 41.

9. Demosthenes 57 *Against Euboulides* 68–69.

10. Apollodoros' presentation of these events suggests but does not imply that Phrastor's illness followed the out-of-court resolution of his dispute with Stephanos, and that is what I am assuming here.

11. Apollodoros says that Phrastor was childless (§55), which may mean either that he had no children at all or that he had no legitimate children. On the order of inheritance within families see Harrison 1968, 144–149; MacDowell 1978, 98–99.

12. On the oikos and the importance of preserving it see Lacey 1968, 96–99; MacDowell 1978, 84–86; Todd 1993, 204–210; Kapparis 1999, 286–287.

13. Isaeus 2 *On the Estate of Menekles* 10, 7 *On the Estate of Apollodoros* 30.

14. [Demosthenes] 46 *Against Stephanos II* 14.

15. Apollodoros tells us that the gennetai rejected Phano's son, but he does not say what the reaction of the phratry members was. Evidently Phrastor's genos was a subgroup within his phratry, and the decision of the genos to reject the boy implied his rejection also from the larger body. See Lambert 1993, 68.

16. In doubting that the public arbitrator decided in favor of the genos, I am following the excellent arguments of Kapparis 1999, 35–36 and 289–293.

17. Cf. Patteson 1978, 95–96; Lambert 1993, 170–171.

18. For discussion of the authenticity of the deposition see Carey 1992, 118; Kapparis 1999, 292–293. Hekale and the other place-names mentioned in the text are demes.

19. The argument is made by Kapparis 1999, 290–291.

CHAPTER 6. HOUSEGUESTS AND HUSBANDS

1. Children whose fathers had died, at least, are known to have remained with their father's families. See Harrison (1968, 44–45) on what became of the children of divorced parents (for which there is very little evidence).

2. Kapparis (1999, 301) guesses at a date of c. 350 for the Epainetos incident.
3. For discussion of Stephanos' vulnerability to future prosecution see Carey 1992, 119; Kapparis 1999, 309.
4. A document has been preserved in our text of Apollodoros' speech which purports to record the terms of reconciliation arrived at on this occasion. In addition to the 1,000-drachma payment Apollodoros mentions in his narrative, this document claims that Stephanos agreed "to make Phano available to Epainetos whenever he was in Athens and wanted to have sex with her" (§71). I agree with Kapparis (1999, 316–317) that this clause (reminiscent of and perhaps inspired by the terms of Stephanos' agreement with Phrynion [§47]) cannot possibly be historical. As events showed, Stephanos was interested in marrying Phano off to a suitable Athenian husband. He could not have expected to find a man for her if she was regularly giving her favors to Epainetos. See Patteson (1978, 102), however, who suggests that the arbitrators viewed Phano as a hetaira. Patterson (1994, 209), too, accepts without question the historicity of the "peculiar private settlement" attested in the document.
5. [Aristotle], *Constitution of Athens* 57.
6. [Aristotle], *Constitution of Athens* 8.1; Hansen 1991, 231. The Athenians selected by lot or elected some 1,100 officials every year, among them a key group of nine men: the eponymous archon (by whose name the year was identified), the archon basileus, the polemarch, and the six thesmothetai. Ancient authors refer to this group as "the nine archons" or simply as "the archons."
7. [Aristotle], *Constitution of Athens* 55; Hansen 1991, 218–220. Kapparis (1999, 320) provides an explanation for the double dokimasia of the nine archons: "Apart from tradition there was a practical reason why a double scrutiny should be retained throughout the classical period: a more careful examination of the eligibility of the nine archons was necessary because at the end of their office they would join the Areopagos [an august council, composed of those who had formerly served as one of the nine archons, which enjoyed certain judicial responsibilities] for life." Cf. Lysias 26 *On the dokimasia of Evandros* 11–12. We will hear more about the Areopagos later in this chapter. See [Aristotle], *Constitution of Athens*, 57.3; MacDowell 1963, 39–47; Wallace 1985, 97–121.
8. The Greek of §72 is clear in suggesting that Phano's marriage to

Theogenes postdated his dokimasia and Stephanos' appointment as paredros. Carey (1992, 122), however, suggests that Theogenes married Phano prior to his dokimasia.

9. Readers will perhaps have heard of these statues in connection with a dark episode in Athens' history. Shortly before the Athenian expedition to Syracuse was to set sail in 415, most of the herms throughout Athens were smashed during a single night, their faces mutilated and their phalluses lopped off. This large-scale act of vandalism, an outrage against the gods and an unfavorable omen for the campaign in Sicily, led to a series of accusations, arrests, and executions. See Thucydides 6.27–29, with Gomme, Andrewes, and Dover 1970, 264–288. See Kapparis (1999, 324–331) for discussion of and bibliography on the Anthesteria. See also Hamilton (1992, 53–54), who argues that the marriage of the basilinna to Dionysos did not occur during the Anthesteria.

10. Develin (1989, 290) suggests that Theogenes served as basileus in the early 360s, but this is probably too early. On the Areopagites' motives in hushing up the scandal see Wallace 1985, 108–109; Kapparis 1999, 350.

11. Were candidates for the office of king archon *required* to have wives who conformed to the model prescribed by the law? If so, a candidate would not only have to pass muster in his own person for the archonship, being ready with all the right answers about his citizenship and military service and so on at his dokimasia, but his suitability for the position would depend also on the status of his wife. He would have to be married, or to become married, to a citizen woman who was neither a widow nor a divorcée (and who, ideally, was not so inconsiderate as to die before she had fulfilled her obligations as basilinna of the year). The effect of this requirement would have been to reduce the number of candidates who were qualified for the office of basileus, making that archonship more selective than the average office that was filled by sortition. We may wonder in that case whether questions about a candidate's wife were raised at his dokimasia. (Spouses are not mentioned in the brief account of a scrutiny interrogation we have at *Constitution of Athens* 55.3.) On the other hand, if the wife of the king archon *did* happen to die prior to the Anthesteria, we may imagine that there was some way out of the difficulty she had thereby caused—some respectable matron from the archon's family may have been hustled in, for example, to play the part of the basilinna at the festival. If so, perhaps

the same fix was possible also in the case of archons whose wives had not been virginal brides, so that marriage to the wrong woman did not in fact disqualify a candidate from the office.

12. On the authenticity of Theogenes' deposition see Carey 1992, 126–128; Kapparis 1999, 351–353.

13. Harrison 1971, 105; MacDowell 1978, 190–191; Carey 1992, 126; Kapparis 1999, 38–39.

14. Aeschines 1 *Against Timarchos* 183.

CHAPTER 7. THE FEUD

1. For discussion of "litigation as feud" see Cohen 1995, 87–118. See also Johnstone (1998). Athenian litigiousness was lampooned on the comic stage. When, for example, the character Strepsiades in Aristophanes' *Clouds* is shown the city of Athens on a map of the world, he is incredulous. "What do you mean? I don't believe it. I don't see any jurors in session" (206–208). Athens would not have been Athens without its lawsuits.

2. For the Athenian expeditions to Olynthus see Carter 1971, 418–429. On Philip's reign see Borza 1990, 198–230. See the orator Demosthenes' Olynthiac orations (speeches 1–3 in the Demosthenic corpus) for his appeals to the Athenians to defend Olynthus more aggressively.

3. Libanius, *Hypothesis to Demosthenes I*, 5. For discussion of the Theoric fund see, for example, Hansen 1976b; Carey 1992, 152–156; Trevett 1992, 138–146; Kapparis 1999, 174–178.

4. See Macurdy (1942, 264), for example, for the suggestion that Apollodoros was acting as a pawn of Demosthenes when he introduced the decree.

5. Hansen (1976b, 237 n. 11) is careful to distinguish the Athenians' vote on Apollodoros' decree from the later vote which the enactment of his decree prompted.

6. On the graphe paranomon see Hansen 1991, 205–212.

7. So Carey 1992, 155. On public debtors see Hunter 2000.

8. Plato, *Apology* 37d.

9. The picture that emerges is that Apollodoros was acting in concert with or on behalf of Demosthenes, and Stephanos was acting for Euboulos. On these political pairings see Trevett 1992, 146–147.

10. For the suggested date of Stephanos' murder charge see Kapparis 1999, 184. One of the actions that initiated a prosecution for mur-

der was a public proclamation in which the alleged murderer was named by one of the victim's relatives (or in this case, as we will see, by the victim's former master). In the proclamation the murderer was ordered to "keep away from legal things" (Antiphon 6 *On the Choreutes* 35–36), in other words, to stay clear of places forbidden him, as a suspected murderer, by law—holy places, courts of law, the agora. The proclamation "was practically equivalent to a public announcement of the prosecution which would follow" (so MacDowell 1963, 24–25). We cannot know why Stephanos disguised his witnesses as Kyreneans. Stephanos may not have wanted the court to know that the witnesses he was presenting—who were perhaps manifestly non-Greek—were slaves. But why Kyrene was selected as their country of origin is not clear. Cf. MacDowell 1963, 107–108.

11. For trials out-of-doors, see Antiphon 5 *On the Murder of Herodes* 11. On intentional homicide see Loomis 1972, especially 92–94. For the different homicide courts see [Aristotle], *Constitution of Athens* 57.3 with Rhodes 1981, 641–644; Demosthenes 23 *Against Aristokrates* 71–73; MacDowell 1963, 44–47, 58–69; Harrison 1971, 36–43.

12. According to Plutarch, *Pericles* 10.6, Pericles was appointed by the state to act as the prosecutor in Kimon's trial of 463 (Hansen 1975, catalogue no. 5; Hamel 1998, 141 no. 3). On public prosecutors see MacDowell 1978, 61–62. See also Bers (forthcoming) on Demosthenes 57 *Against Euboulides:* the Athenians sometimes revised their citizen registers, deme by deme, in order to remove from the lists foreigners or metics who had managed to insinuate themselves. Anyone who was struck from the register could appeal the decision, and in the resulting court case the deme was represented by accusers elected by the demesmen. On the prosecution of murderers by slave owners see MacDowell 1963, 17–21; Tulin 1996, 18 n. 43, 101–106.

13. Most manuscripts of the text read "from 500 drachmas," though many editors have deleted "drachmas" and understood the passage to refer to 500 jurors. For discussion see, for example, Kapparis 1999, 187–189; MacDowell 1963, 55. The passage may mean that Stephanos received 500 drachmas to bring the case against Apollodoros or that he spent 500 drachmas on suborning witnesses for the trial. That there was in fact no woman murdered in Aphidna is the conclusion of Kapparis 1999, 182–183.

14. Demosthenes 18 *On the Crown* 21, 19 *On the False Embassy* 168. Aeschines 2 *On the Embassy* 140. For discussion of the political background to the murder trial see Trevett 1992, 148–149; Kapparis 1999, 183–184.
15. On the virtues of *apragmosyne*—non-meddlesomeness—in Athens see Lateiner 1982; Carter 1986, 106–113.
16. For discussion see Hansen 1991, 194–196; Carey 1992, 84; Cohen 1995, 66–72, 83–84, and 102–106; Christ 1998, 154–157.
17. On Apollodoros' assets see Davies 1971, 442: "even making allowance for Apollodoros' extravagance, his claim that his property was worth less than 3 *tal.* in 349/8 ([Dem.] lix. 7) is little short of preposterous." See also Trevett 1992, 27–31.
18. For discussion of the political dimension of the trial see Macurdy 1942; Carey 1992, 6–8; Trevett 1992, 149–150; Kapparis 1999, 30–31. On vengeance in Athens see Herman 2000.

CHAPTER 8. SUPPORTING CHARACTERS

1. Demosthenes 45 *Against Stephanos I* 55, 50 *Against Polykles* 24. Davies 1971, 437, 441; Trevett 1992, 19. On marriage between relatives see Harrison 1968, 21–24.
2. [Demosthenes] 46 *Against Stephanos II* 26. For the widespread use of synegoroi in public suits see Rubinstein 2000, 78–80 and 91–111. See also MacDowell 1978, 250–251; Todd 1993, 94–95.
3. See Trevett (1992, 64) for the number of words in the *Against Neaira*. The figure does not include the text of the documents inserted into the speech. English translations of Greek prose are apt to be more wordy than the originals, since, for one thing, the Greeks could pack a lot of information into a single participle. To give a sense of the length of the speech in English, Bers's translation (including the documents) comes to roughly 13,000 words.
4. Hansen 1976a, 63–66. On the reasons for Theomnestos' role in the case see Patteson 1978, 6; Kapparis 1999, 196–197.
5. In §§94–106 of the speech Apollodoros discusses the Athenians' mass enfrachisement of the Plataeans, residents of Plataea in southern Boeotia, after their town was razed by the Spartans in 427. (The Spartans later built a hotel on the site.) Among other examples of the loyalty to their allies which won the Plataeans Athenian citizenship was their contribution at the Battle of Marathon in 490.

The Plataeans were the only Greeks who came to the assistance of the Athenians on that occasion, helping them drive from Attic soil the Persian forces that were bent on destroying Athens. Apollodoros contrasts Stephanos' de facto deferment of citizenship on people unworthy of the honor with the Plataeans' services to Athens and the care the Athenians took in enfranchising them, scrutinizing each candidate individually lest faux-Plataeans be mistakenly admitted to the Athenian fold.

6. This account of the history of Apollodoros and his family owes much to Trevett 1992, 1–49. See also Isager and Hansen 1975, 180–190.

7. Demosthenes 45 *Against Stephanos I* 85. We do not know what status Archippe enjoyed after her husband's enfranchisement. For discussion of the question see Whitehead 1986a; Sealey 1990, 18–19; Carey 1991.

8. Demosthenes 36 *For Phormion* 22. See Trevett (1992, 165–179) on Apollodoros' attempts to embrace the lifestyle and ideology of wealthy Athenians by, for example, involving himself in the city's political life. For the case against Kallippos see Trevett 1992, 9 and 126.

9. Trevett 1992, 9–10, 32–33, and 126–127. On piracy and human spoils see Casson 1991, 178. Apollodoros' *Against Nikostratos* is preserved as [Demosthenes] 53.

10. Demosthenes 36 *For Phormion* 41. Trevett 1992, 11 and 127–129.

11. On Apollodoros' feud with Phormion see Trevett 1992, 6–15.

12. Demosthenes 45 *Against Stephanos I* 30, 71–86.

13. On the trierarchy see in general Gabrielsen 1994. *Leitourgia*, or "liturgy," literally means a public service. The same word came to refer to the official public services of the Christian Church, and more particularly, especially in the Eastern Church, to the sacrament of the Eucharist. On liturgies see MacDowell 1978, 161–164; Hansen 1991, 110–112.

14. Demosthenes 45 *Against Stephanos I* 78. See Trevett 1992, 11–14 and 36–38.

15. Demosthenes 36 *For Phormion* 53.

16. Harrison 1971, 47 with n. 2; Hansen 1991, 187. In practice it was possible for jurors, at least in small numbers, not to cast votes, in which case the addition of the tie-breaking odd juror would not help matters. Tie votes, however, meant a verdict for the defendant. See Harrison (1971, 47 with n. 3) and Todd (1993, 83 n. 10) for

discussion. On the Athenian courts generally see Hansen 1991, 178–224.

17. [Aristotle], *Constitution of Athens* 63.4; Kroll 1972; Rhodes 1981, 704; Boegehold 1995, 59–61.

18. [Aristotle], *Constitution of Athens* 62.2. Aristophanes, *Wasps* 230–239, 300–311. For the number of court days per year see Hansen 1979 and 1991, 186. On the age of jurors see Rhodes 1981, 691; Hansen 1991, 185–186.

19. For discussion of the procedure see, for example, Moore 1975, 303–307; Rhodes 1981, 700–717; Hansen 1991, 197–199. Bers (2000) argues that the complexity of the procedure served also to imbue the experience with a certain solemnity, which in turn would have inspired confidence in the process.

20. On the kleroteria see Boegehold 1995, 230–231.

21. For the number of citizens eligible for jury service in the fourth century see Hansen 1991, 91 and 181.

22. Aeschines 1 *Against Timarchos* 2. The jurors may have sworn this oath in the case of private speeches only. For discussion see Rhodes 1981, 718–719.

23. [Aristotle], *Constitution of Athens*, 67. Harrison 1971, 161–163; Rhodes 1981, 719–728; Hansen 1991, 187–188. Mogens Hansen (1991, 199) guesses that the entire allotment procedure, including the selection of the ten jurors inside the courtroom, took no more than an hour.

24. Rhodes 1981, 720; Boegehold 1995, 77–78. Among the courtesans of Neaira's day was a certain Metiche, nicknamed Klepsydra. She got the sobriquet, allegedly, from timing her sexual encounters with a water clock: when the water ran dry, her gentleman caller's time was up (Athenaeus, *Dinner-sophists* 567c–d).

25. On courtroom interruptions see Bers 1985, 6–12.

26. On voting ballots see Boegehold 1995, 82–86. For the voting procedure see [Aristotle], *Constitution of Athens* 68; Rhodes 1981, 730–733; Hansen 1991, 202–203. Given the length of the litigants' speeches, readers will perhaps be wondering about the logistics of mid-trial dicastic excretion. To my knowledge, the details elude us. A chamber pot plays a role in the mock courtroom of Aristophanes' *Wasps* (lines 807–808, 935), but this may not reflect an excretory reality. In his article on Athens' *koprologoi* (dung-collectors), Owens (1983) has a bit to say about domestic facilities (cf. Olson 1998, 87), but he suggests that very little is known about toilets in Athens in

general. (It is worth mentioning that in his comic play *Birds* [790–792] Aristophanes refers to a politician named Patrokleides who, the passage suggests, was famous in Athens for having once soiled himself in public—a sorry thing to be known for millennia after the fact: "And if some Patrokleides among you happens to have to go, he would not ooze into his cloak but would [being a bird] fly off." The ability to fly away in such circumstances is, according to the chorus in the play, one of the advantages of being a bird. On the passage see Dunbar 1995, 482.)

CHAPTER 9. NEAIRA'S TRIAL

1. See Carey (1992, 112), however, on the inadequacy of the polemarch's involvement as a proof of Neaira's status.
2. As we have seen, Apollodoros puts the stories of Phano's two marriages to a second use as well, adducing them as proof that Stephanos was living in a marriage relationship with Neaira. Apollodoros only makes this argument at the very end of his speech, however, not while he is telling Phano's story to the jurors.
3. This sentence, Proustian in its length, is a good example of Apollodoros' tendency to pile on clauses. In order to give a better sense of the style of the Greek I have elected not to break my translation of his 147-word sentence into shorter segments.
4. The Greek for "from three holes" is mentioned as belonging to the text by Hermogenes, who wrote on Greek prose style in the second century A.D. Apollodoros, however, may not in fact have used the coarse expression in court. The phrase does not appear in any manuscript of the speech.
5. Demosthenes 24 *Against Timokrates* 151.
6. For discussion of Apollodoros' history see Trevett 1992, 151.

WORKS CITED

I have not attempted to provide complete bibliography for any of the numerous subjects touched on in this book. Readers interested in investigating topics in greater detail are urged to consult the relevant passages in the commentaries by Konstantinos Kapparis and Christopher Carey for more extensive discussion and citations.

PERIODICAL ABBREVIATIONS

ABSA Annual of the British School at Athens
AJP American Journal of Philology
CJ Classical Journal
ClAnt Classical Antiquity
CQ Classical Quarterly
CW Classical World
EMC Echos du Monde Classique
GRBS Greek, Roman, and Byzantine Studies
JHS Journal of Hellenic Studies
LCM Liverpool Classical Monthly
PCPS Proceedings of the Cambridge Philological Society
PP La Parola del Passato
RIDA Revue internationale des droits de l'antiquité
TAPA Transactions of the American Philological Association
ZSS Zeitschrift der Savigny-Stiftung für Rechstgeschichte, romanistische Abteilung

Anderson, J. K. 1970. *Military Theory and Practice in the Age of Xenophon.* Berkeley: University of California Press.

Bers, Victor. 1985. "Dikastic *Thorubos.*" In *Crux: Essays Presented to G. E. M. de Ste. Croix on His 75th Birthday,* ed. P. A. Cartledge and F. D. Harvey. Exeter, England: Imprint Academic, 1–15.

———. 1997. *Speech in Speech: Studies in Incorporated Oratio Recta in Attic Drama and Oratory.* Lanham, Md.: Rowman and Little-field.

———. 2000. "Just Rituals: Why the Rigmarole of Fourth-Century Athenian Lawcourts?" In *Polis and Politics,* ed. Pernille Flensted-Jensen, Thomas Heine Nielsen, and Lene Rubinstein, 553–562. Copenhagen: Museum Tusculanum Press.

Bers, Victor, trans. Forthcoming. *Demosthenes: Speeches 50–59.* Austin: University of Texas Press.

Boegehold, Alan L. 1995. *The Lawcourts at Athens: Sites, Buildings, Equipment, Procedure, and Testimonia.* Vol. 28 of *The Athenian Agora.* Princeton: American School of Classical Studies at Athens.

Boegehold, Alan L., and Adele Scafuro, eds. 1994. *Athenian Identity and Civic Ideology.* Baltimore: Johns Hopkins University Press.

Borza, Eugene N. 1990. *In the Shadow of Olympus.* Princeton: Princeton University Press.

Breitenbach, Hermann. 1908. "De genere quodam titulorum comoediae atticae." Ph.D. diss., Basel.

Buck, Robert J. 1998. *Thrasybulus and the Athenian Democracy.* Stuttgart: Franz Steiner Verlag.

Cameron, Averil, and Amélie Kuhrt, eds. 1983. *Images of Women in Antiquity.* Detroit: Wayne State University Press.

Cantarella, Eva. 1987. *Pandora's Daughters.* Baltimore: Johns Hopkins University Press.

Carey, Christopher. 1991. "Apollodoros' Mother: The Wives of Enfranchised Aliens in Athens." *CQ* 41, 84–89.

———. 1992. *Apollodoros Against Neaira [Demosthenes] 59.* Warminster, England: Aris & Phillips.

———. 1993. "Return of the Radish *or* Just When You Thought It Was Safe to Go Back into the Kitchen." *LCM* 18.4, 53–55.

———. 1997. *Trials from Classical Athens.* London: Routledge.

Carter, John M. 1971. "Athens, Euboea, and Olynthus." *Historia* 20, 418–429.

Carter, L. B. 1986. *The Quiet Athenian.* Oxford: Oxford University Press.

Cartledge, Paul. 1981. "Spartan Wives: Liberation or License?" *CQ* 31, 84–105.

WORKS CITED

———. 1987. *Agesilaos and the Crisis of Sparta*. Baltimore: Johns Hopkins University Press.

Cartledge, Paul, Paul Millett, and Stephen Todd, eds. 1990. *Nomos: Essays in Athenian Law, Politics, and Society*. Cambridge: Cambridge University Press.

Casson, Lionel. 1991. *The Ancient Mariners*. Princeton: Princeton University Press.

Christ, Matthew R. 1998. *The Litigious Athenian*. Baltimore: Johns Hopkins University Press.

Cohen, David. 1985. "A Note on Aristophanes and the Punishment of Adultery in Athenian Law." *ZSS* 102, 385–387.

———. 1991. *Law, Sexuality, and Society*. Cambridge: Cambridge University Press.

———. 1995. *Law, Violence and Community in Classical Athens*. Cambridge: Cambridge University Press.

Cohen, Edward E. 1992. *Athenian Economy and Society*. Princeton: Princeton University Press.

Cohen, Patricia Cline. 1998. *The Murder of Helen Jewett*. New York: Alfred A. Knopf.

Cohn-Haft, L. 1995. "Divorce in Classical Athens." *JHS* 115, 1–14.

Cox, Cheryl Anne. 1998. *Household Interests: Property, Marriage Strategies, and Family Dynamics in Ancient Athens*. Princeton: Princeton University Press.

Davidson, James. 1997. *Courtesans and Fishcakes*. London: HarperCollins.

Davies, J. K. 1971. *Athenian Propertied Families, 600–300 B.C.* Oxford: Oxford University Press.

Develin, Robert. 1989. *Athenian Officials, 684–321 B.C.* Cambridge: Cambridge University Press.

Dover, K. J. 1968a. *Aristophanes: Clouds*. Oxford: Oxford University Press.

———. 1968b. *Lysias and the Corpus Lysiacum*. Berkeley: University of California Press.

———. 1974. *Greek Popular Morality in the Time of Plato and Aristotle*. Oxford: Basil Blackwell.

———. 1978. *Greek Homosexuality*. New York: Vintage Books.

———. 1984. "Classical Greek Attitudes to Sexual Behavior." In *Women in the Ancient World*, ed. John Peradotto and J. P. Sullivan. Albany: State University of New York Press. 145–157.

DuBois, Page. 1991. *Torture and Truth*. New York: Routledge.

Dunbar, Nan. 1995. *Aristophanes: Birds*. Oxford: Oxford University Press.

Edwards, M. J. 1999. *Lysias: Five Speeches*. London: Bristol Classical Press.

Flensted-Jensen, Pernille, Thomas Heine Nielsen, and Lene Rubinstein, eds. 2000. *Polis and Politics*. Copenhagen: Museum Tusculanum Press.

Gabrielsen, Vincent. 1994. *Financing the Athenian Fleet*. Baltimore: Johns Hopkins University Press.

Garlan, Yvon. 1988. *Slavery in Ancient Greece*. Trans. Janet Lloyd. Ithaca, N.Y.: Cornell University Press.

Garland, Robert. 1990. *The Greek Way of Life*. Ithaca, N.Y.: Cornell University Press.

Gill, Christopher. 1973. "The Death of Socrates." *CQ* 23, 25–28.

Gomme, A. W., A. Andrewes, and K. J. Dover. 1970. *A Historical Commentary on Thucydides*. Vol. 4. Oxford: Clarendon Press.

Gould, John. 1980. "Law, Custom and Myth: Aspects of the Social Position of Women in Classical Athens." *JHS* 100, 38–59.

Gow, A. S. F., ed. 1965. *Machon: The Fragments*. Cambridge: Cambridge University Press.

Graham, A. J. 1998. "The Woman at the Window: Observations on the 'Stele from the Harbour' of Thasos." *JHS* 118, 22–40.

Hamel, Debra. 1998. *Athenian Generals: Military Authority in the Classical Period*. Leiden: Brill Academic Publishers.

Hamilton, Charles D. 1997. "Sparta." In *The Greek World in the Fourth Century*, ed. Lawrence A. Tritle. London: Routledge. 41–65.

Hamilton, R. 1992. *Choes and Anthesteria: Athenian Iconography and Ritual*. Ann Arbor: University of Michigan Press.

Hansen, Mogens Herman. 1975. *Eisangelia: The Sovereignty of the People's Court in Athens in the Fourth Century B.C. and the Impeachment of Generals and Politicians*. Odense: Odense University Press.

———. 1976a. *Apagoge, Endeixis and Ephegesis Against Kakourgoi, Atimoi and Pheugontes*. Odense: Odense University Press.

———. 1976b. "The Theoric Fund and the *Graphe Paranomon* Against Apollodorus." *GRBS* 17, 235–246.

———. 1979. "How Often Did the Athenian *Dicasteria* Meet?" *GRBS* 20, 243–246.

———. 1991. *The Athenian Democracy in the Age of Demosthenes*. Oxford: Basil Blackwell.

Hanson, Victor Davis. 1998. *Warfare and Agriculture in Classical Greece.*
Rev. ed. Berkeley: University of California Press.

Harrison, A. R. W. 1968. *The Law of Athens.* Vol. 1. 2nd ed. London:
Bristol Classical Press.

———. 1971. *The Law of Athens.* Vol. 2. 2nd ed. London: Bristol
Classical Press.

Harvey, David. 1990. "The Sykophant and Sykophancy: Vexatious
Redefinition?" In *Nomos: Essays in Athenian Law, Politics, and
Society,* ed. Paul Cartledge, Paul Millett, and Stephen Todd.
Cambridge: Cambridge University Press. 103–121.

Henderson, Jeffrey. 1975. *The Maculate Muse.* New Haven: Yale
University Press.

Herman, G. 2000. "Athenian Beliefs About Revenge: Problems and
Methods." *PCPS* 46, 7–27.

Hunter, Virginia. 1994. *Policing Athens: Social Control in the Attic
Lawsuits, 420–320 B.C.* Princeton: Princeton University Press.

———. 2000. "Policing Public Debtors in Classical Athens." *Phoenix*
54, 21–38.

Isager, Signe, and Mogens Herman Hansen. 1975. *Aspects of Athenian
Society in the Fourth Century B.C.* Odense: Odense University Press.

Johnstone, Steven. 1998. "Cracking the Code of Silence: Athenian
Legal Oratory and the Histories of Slaves and Women." In *Women
and Slaves in Greco-Roman Culture,* ed. Sheila Murnaghan and
Sandra R. Joshel. London: Routledge. 221–236.

Just, Roger. 1989. *Women in Athenian Law and Life.* London:
Routledge.

Kapparis, K. 1996. "Humiliating the Adulterer: The Law and the
Practice in Classical Athens." *RIDA* 43, 63–77.

———. 1999. *Apollodoros "Against Neaira" [D. 59].* Berlin: Walter de
Gruyter.

Kassel, R., and C. Austin, eds. 1983–2001. *Poetae Comici Graeci.*
Berlin: Walter de Gruyter. Referred to in the notes as K-A.

Katz, Marilyn A. 1994. "Ideology and the 'Status of Women' in
Ancient Greece." In *Feminists Revision History,* ed. Ann-Louise
Shapiro. New Brunswick, N.J.: Rutgers University Press. 120–145.

Keuls, Eva C. 1985. *The Reign of the Phallus.* New York: Harper & Row.

Kilmer, Martin F. 1982. "Genital Phobia and Depilation." *JHS* 102,
104–112.

———. 1993. *Greek Erotica on Attic Red-Figure Vases.* London:
Duckworth.

Krenkel, Werner A. 1988. "Prostitution." In *Civilization of the Ancient Mediterranean.* Vol 2. Ed. Michael Grant and Rachel Kitzinger. New York: Charles Scribner's Sons. 1291–1297.

Krentz, Peter. 1982. *The Thirty at Athens.* Ithaca, N.Y.: Cornell University Press.

Kroll, J. H. 1972. *Athenian Bronze Allotment Plates.* Cambridge, Mass.: Harvard University Press.

Kurke, Leslie. 1997. "Inventing the Hetaira: Sex, Politics, and Discursive Conflict in Archaic Greece." *ClAnt* 16, 106–150.

Lacey, W. K. 1968. *The Family in Classical Greece.* Ithaca, N.Y.: Cornell University Press.

Lambert, S. D. 1993. *The Phratries of Attica.* Ann Arbor: University of Michigan Press.

Lateiner, Donald. 1982. "'The Man Who Does Not Meddle in Politics': A *Topos* in Lysias." *CW* 76, 1–12.

Lefkowitz, Mary. 1983. "Influential Women." In *Images of Women in Antiquity,* ed. Averil Cameron and Amélie Kuhrt. Detroit: Wayne State University Press. 49–64.

Lewis, Sian. 1996. *News and Society in the Greek Polis.* Chapel Hill: University of North Carolina Press.

Loomis, William T. 1972. "The Nature of Premeditation in Athenian Homicide Law." *JHS* 92, 86–95.

———. 1998. *Wages, Welfare Costs, and Inflation in Classical Athens.* Ann Arbor: University of Michigan Press.

MacDowell, Douglas M. 1963. *Athenian Homicide Law.* Manchester, England: Manchester University Press.

———. 1978. *The Law in Classical Athens.* London: Thames and Hudson.

Macurdy, Grace H. 1942. "Apollodorus and the Speech Against Neaira (Pseudo-Dem. LIX)." *AJP* 63, 257–271.

Martin, Thomas R. 1985. *Sovereignty and Coinage in Classical Greece.* Princeton: Princeton University Press.

Millett, P. 1991. *Lending and Borrowing in Ancient Athens.* Cambridge: Cambridge University Press.

Mirhady, David C. 1996. "Torture and Rhetoric in Athens." *JHS* 116, 119–131.

Moore, J. M. 1975. *Aristotle and Xenophon on Democracy and Oligarchy.* Berkeley: University of California Press.

Morris, Ian. 1998. "Remaining Invisible: The Archaeology of the Excluded in Classical Athens." In *Women and Slaves in Greco-Roman*

Culture, ed. Sheila Murnaghan and Sandra R. Joshel. London: Routledge. 193–221.

Munn, Mark H. 1993. *The Defense of Attica.* Berkeley: University of California Press.

Murnaghan, Sheila, and Sandra R. Joshel. 1998. *Women and Slaves in Greco-Roman Culture.* London: Routledge.

Nails, Debra. 1998. "The Dramatic Date of Plato's *Republic.*" *CJ* 93.4, 383–396.

Navarre, O. 1904. "Meretrices." *Dictionnaire des antiquités grecques et romaines.* Paris: Libraire Hachette.

Nevett, L. C. 1995. "Gender Relations in the Classical Greek Household: The Archaeological Evidence." *ABSA* 90, 363–381.

Ober, Josiah. 1989. *Mass and Elite in Democratic Athens.* Princeton: Princeton University Press.

Olson, S. Douglas. 1998. *Aristophanes: Peace.* Oxford: Oxford University Press.

Osborne, Robin. 1990. "Vexatious Litigation in Classical Athens: Sykophancy and the Sykophant." In *Nomos: Essays in Athenian Law, Politics, and Society,* ed. Paul Cartledge, Paul Millett, and Stephen Todd. Cambridge: Cambridge University Press. 83–102.

Owens, E. J. 1983. "The Koprologoi at Athens in the Fifth and Fourth Centuries B.C." *CQ* 33.1, 44–50.

Parke, H. W. 1977. *Festivals of the Athenians.* Ithaca, N.Y.: Cornell University Press.

Parker, Holt N. 1992. "Love's Body Anatomized: The Ancient Erotic Handbooks and the Rhetoric of Sexuality." In *Pornography and Representation in Greece and Rome,* ed. Amy Richlin. New York: Oxford University Press. 90–111.

Patterson, Cynthia. 1985. " 'Not Worth the Rearing': The Causes of Infant Exposure in Ancient Greece." *TAPA* 115, 103–123.

———. 1991. "Marriage and the Married Woman in Athenian Law." In *Women's History and Ancient History,* ed. Sarah B. Pomeroy. Chapel Hill: University of North Carolina Press. 48–72.

———. 1994. "The Case Against Neaira and the Public Ideology of the Athenian Family." In *Athenian Identity and Civic Ideology,* ed. Alan L. Boegehold and Adele Scafuro. Baltimore: Johns Hopkins University Press. 199–216.

———. 1998. *The Family in Greek History.* Cambridge, Mass.: Harvard University Press.

Patteson, Alice Jean. 1978. "Commentary on [Demosthenes] LIX: Against Neaera." Ph.D. diss., University of Pennsylvania.

Pearson, Lionel. 1966. "Apollodorus, the Eleventh Attic Orator." In *The Classical Tradition,* ed. Luitpold Wallach. Ithaca, N.Y.: Cornell University Press. 347–359.

Pomeroy, Sarah B. 1975. *Goddesses, Whores, Wives, and Slaves: Women in Classical Antiquity.* New York: Schocken Books.

———. 1983. "Infanticide in Hellenistic Greece." In *Images of Women in Antiquity,* ed. Averil Cameron and Amélie Kuhrt. Detroit: Wayne State University Press. 207–222.

Porter, John R. 1997. "Adultery by the Book: Lysias I (*On the Murder of Eratosthenes*) and Comic *Diegesis*." *EMC* 40 n.s. 16, 421–453.

Rhodes, P. J. 1981. *A Commentary on the Aristotelian Athenaion Politeia.* Oxford: Clarendon Press.

Riddle, John M. 1992. *Contraception and Abortion from the Ancient World to the Renaissance.* Cambridge, Mass.: Harvard University Press.

Roy, J. 1991. "Traditional Jokes About the Punishment of Adulterers in Ancient Greek Literature." *LCM* 16.5, 73–76.

Rubinstein, Lene. 2000. *Litigation and Cooperation: Supporting Speakers in the Courts of Classical Athens. Historia Einzelschriften* 147. Stuttgart: Steiner.

Sage, Michael M. 1996. *Warfare in Ancient Greece: A Sourcebook.* London: Routledge.

Scafuro, Adele C. 1994. "Witnessing and False Witnessing: Proving Citizenship and Kin Identity in Fourth-Century Athens." In *Athenian Identity and Civic Ideology,* ed. Alan L. Boegehold and Adele Scafuro. Baltimore: Johns Hopkins University Press. 156–198.

———. 1997. *The Forensic Stage.* Cambridge: Cambridge University Press.

Schaps, David. 1977. "The Woman Least Mentioned: Etiquette and Women's Names." *CQ* 71, 323–330.

Sealey, Raphael. 1956. "Callistratos of Aphidna and his Contemporaries." *Historia* 5, 178–203.

———. 1990. *Women and Law in Classical Greece.* Chapel Hill: University of North Carolina Press.

Slater, Philip E. 1968. *The Glory of Hera.* Boston: Beacon Press.

Starr, Chester G. 1978. "An Evening with the Flute-Girls." *PP* 33, 401–410.

Thur, Gerhard. 1996. "Reply to D. C. Mirhady, 'Torture and Rhetoric in Athens.'" *JHS* 116, 132–134.

Todd, S. C. 1993. *The Shape of Athenian Law*. Oxford: Clarendon Press.

———. 2000. *Lysias*. Austin: University of Texas Press.

Traill, John S. 1975. *The Political Organization of Attica. Hesperia.* Supplement 14. Princeton: American School of Classical Studies at Athens.

Trevett, Jeremy. 1992. *Apollodoros the Son of Pasion*. Oxford: Clarendon Press.

Tulin, Alexander. 1996. *Dike Phonou: The Right of Prosecution and Attic Homicide Procedure*. Stuttgart: B. G. Teubner.

Ussher, R. G. 1973: *Aristophanes Ecclesiazusae*. Oxford: Oxford University Press.

Walker, Susan. 1983. "Women and Housing in Classical Greece: The Archaeological Evidence." In *Images of Women in Antiquity*, ed. Averil Cameron and Amélie Kuhrt. Detroit: Wayne State University Press. 81–91.

Wallace, Robert. 1985. *The Areopagos Council to 307 B.C.* Baltimore: Johns Hopkins University Press.

———. 2000. "'Investigations and Reports' by the Areopagos Council and Demosthenes' Areopagos Decree." In *Polis and Politics,* ed. Pernille Flensted-Jensen, Thomas Heine Nielsen, and Lene Rubinstein. Copenhagen: Museum Tusculanum Press. 581–595.

Whitehead, David. 1986a. "Women and Naturalisation in Fourth Century Athens: The Case of Archippe." *CQ* 36, 109–114.

———. 1986b. *The Demes of Attica, 508/7–ca. 250 B.C.* Princeton: Princeton University Press.

———. 2000. *Hypereides: The Forensic Speeches*. Oxford: Oxford University Press.

Wilkinson, L. P. 1978. *Classical Attitudes to Modern Issues*. London: William Kimber.

INDEX

Abortion, 49

Adoption, 87

Adultery. See *Moicheia; Moichoi*

Agones timetoi, 122, 129, 149, 153

Allotment machines, 144–147

Amateurs, Athenian reliance on, xii, 133, 148

Amphidromia, 54

Amsterdam, prostitution in, 164*n5*

Anthesteria, 103–106, 112

Antidorides, 60–61

Apollodoros: self-description, ix; speeches of, xii, 137–140; argumentation of, 49–55, 59–61, 80–81, 89–93, 101, 155–160, 183*n2;* decree on surplus monies, 119–120; *graphe paranomon* against, 121–123, 128–130; finances of, 121, 129–130, 180*n17;* charged with murder, 123–126; reasons for not prosecuting Neaira, 134–135; and Phormion, 138–139; trierarchies of, 140; verbosity of, 172*n18,* 183*n3.*

—*Against Kallippos,* and feud with Kallippos, 137

—*Against Neaira,* authorship of, xii; length of, 134

—*Against Nikostratos,* and feud with Nikostratos, 137–138

—*Against Polykles,* and trierarchy, 140

—*Against Stephanos II,* and feud with Phormion, 139

—*Against Timotheos,* and recovery of debts, 138

Arbitration, 74–76, 91–93, 100–101

Archippe, 136, 138, 181*n7*

Archon basileus, 102–103, 177–178*n11*

Archons: "nine archons," 102, 103, 156, 157, 176*nn6, 7.* See also *Archon basileus*

Areopagos Council, 106–112, 124, 176*n7*

Ariston, 48–49, 52–55, 60

Aristophanes:

—*Birds:* on ornithic excretion, 183*n26*

—*Clouds:* on radishing, 69; on litigiousness, 178*n1*

Wages: of skilled workers, 6–7,
164n6; of jurors, 143, 153–
154, 164n6; of assemblymen,
164n6. *See also* Prices
Witnesses, 41, 54, 61, 84. *See
also* Torture
Women: segregation of, 5–6,
14–15, 26–28; domestic responsibilities of, 14, 165n15;
in Sparta, 14; not mentioned
by name, 28, 168n35; libidinousness of, 79; proof of status of, 84; found with *moichoi*,

100, 111; silent in court, 128,
133; Apollodoros' categorization of, 171n7. *See also* Prostitutes

Xenarchos:
—*Pentathlum:* on brothels, 5, 15
—4K-A: on *moichoi*, 70
Xenokleides, 66–67
Xenophon:
—*Memoirs of Socrates*, on Theo-
dote, 12
—*Symposium*, on symposia, 8–9